# ON SOCIAL CONSTRAINTS AND THE GREAT LONGING

## An Essay on the Human Condition

# ON SOCIAL CONSTRAINTS AND THE GREAT LONGING

## An Essay on the Human Condition

**Avijit Pathak**

*On Social Constraints and the Great Longing*
*An Essay on the Human Condition*
Avijit Pathak



First Published 2014
**Reprinted 2023**

ISBN 978-93-5002-268-9 (Pb)



*Published by*
**AAKAR BOOKS**
28 E Pocket IV, Mayur Vihar Phase I
Delhi 110 091, India
www.aakarbooks.com

*Printed at*
D.K. Fine Art Press, Delhi

# DEDICATION

*"One of our past lives... A tapovan. Quite early in the morning. Distant mountains... a flowing river... I am your guru. You are my disciple, my child. We are reflecting on the Self, on temporality and eternity, on love and death. We are coming back. A small/ beautiful cottage amidst trees. Guruma—the embodiment of beauty, grace and wisdom—is waiting for us with her offering —the food that purifies...*

*2013. A modern university. Yet, an accommodation surrounded by trees, peacocks and birds... The professor's wife has left her physical body. Yet, she is all-pervading. She inspires. The professor enters the kitchen, makes a cup of tea for his student, his child. And then they begin to converse...There is eternal recurrence. Everything, my dear, is connected. Love makes one see...".*

From an invisible diary.

The book is dedicated to the spirit of togetherness.

# PREFACE

There is no academic compulsion, no peer pressure to produce, to write yet another book, to add to the list of publications, and survive in a recklessly competitive/ narcissistic scholarly field. I, therefore, want to caution my readers. Don't see this book as yet another 'product' manufactured by the faculty of a reputed university. Don't search academic chess games. Don't search technicality, formality, coldness, abstraction, the ritualism of academic writing. Instead, let me make it clear, everything relating to this book is about *inspiration*. It is about suffering and struggle, constraints and aspirations, love and prayer. There is no 'method of data collection'; words are wet; words have emerged out of the depths of my soul. The book does not intend to impress the priestcraft of academics. With grey hair and possibly a wrinkled face I have become somewhat free from this anxiety. I have no desire to prove anything. As a matter of fact, I do not write; there is an invisible force that makes me write. The book is a gift of love and inspiration.

Yes, as the reader would find, it begins with *work* and ends with *death*; it passes through *power* and *conflict*, *order* and *chaos*, *desire* and *identity*, *fear* and *love*. In a way the book is about the fundamental questions of existence that each of us confronts. It does not negate the intimacy with one's authentic self; seeing is not just analyzing the world out there; seeing is also an awareness of one's inner treasure. As a result, sociology becomes intimate; self and world are fused; literary imagination embraces sociological reasoning; philosophy does not remain distant; it transforms itself into a song of everyday life; Durkheim, Weber, Marx, Foucault—they all emerge as fellow travellers one loves to associate with; there is no one way traffic of ideas; Gandhi, Aurobindo, Ambedkar and Tagore appear time and again; there is no censorship, no fear of contamination, no exclusion; Marx and *Upanishads* coexist. I invite my readers to this journey, this flow of ideas. I want them to think and feel.

My students bear my madness; they inspire me. With deep gratitude I recall them. With absolute humility I accept their gifts: a cup of lemon tea under a tree, a painting expressing the eternal curiosity of a small child, a discourse on Rumi and Kabir, a piece of musical wonder by Mozart, a guitar with a melodious voice, a flower with its fragrance, a dream, a book on Krishnamurti, unbounded laughter, a telephone call—'Sir, look at the sky, the moon has finally arrived'. My daughter, her eyes that continue to search her invisible, yet truly spirited mother, my loved ones: I bow down, and realize that it is love—not pride—that makes one work. My publisher makes me believe in the virtue of hard work. And finally, I wish to whisper into the ears of my *ideal* reader: 'Even now—in these troubled times—the sun rises, the flower blooms, and the tree converses with the little/lovely bird'.

November 24, 2013

**Avijit Pathak**
Jawaharlal Nehru University
New Delhi

## (I)

There is no escape from *work*. Everyone, it seems, is working. A mother is nurturing her child, working in her kitchen; a father is looking at the office files, dictating notes; a teacher is reading books, delivering lectures; a farmer is sowing seeds in his land; a construction worker is toiling, helping to create skyscrapers; and the story goes on. Looking at the world is like seeing people working day and night. Indeed, the world we live in is characterized by a ceaseless flow of work. It is through work that we engage with the world, we relate to nature, shape it, use it and modulate it. It is through work that we manufacture commodities, cultivate land, produce food grains; it is work that enables us to build roads, flyovers, airports; and it is work that gives us sustenance and livelihood. No wonder, a reflection on the human condition requires an understanding of the domain of work.

It would not be wrong to say that one's state of mind can also be understood through the mode of engagement with work. For some, work is nothing but compulsion; it is not an inner calling; it is for sheer survival. A child working in a roadside dhaba for sixteen hours, or a housewife perpetually fulfilling the orders of an oppressive husband in a patriarchal family—work is nothing but a bondage; it does not radiate positive vibrations; it is boredom, a deep cry from inside. For some, work is primarily for utility, for purely personal gains, for maximizing profit. Even when in the process of this work one engages with others, it remains utilitarian. A real estate agent selling an apartment to a customer, or a management graduate changing jobs every year for a better salary package—work is calculative, instrumental; its success or worth is measured in terms of material gains. But for some, work is a creative accomplishment, a sense of fulfilment of inner urges. A mother preparing the dish her child likes; an inspired poet taking up the pen, and giving birth to rhythmic words; an artist engaged in his studio; a teacher deeply involved in her teaching—work is like a splendid merger of the creator and his/her creation. It generates positivity; it is intrinsically fulfilling; even when it brings money, fame, prosperity, its essence lies in its creative rhythm. And finally, there are some for whom work is an opportunity to expand their horizons, break all barriers, and transcend the otherness of the other. A Gandhi working day and night to arouse the imagination of the nation, a Mother Teresa nursing the destitute—work is deeply cathectic and relational; it restores faith, and creates the foundation of moral communities.

It should not be forgotten that work requires mental and physical energy. Work is labour; work is hardship; work is a constant negotiation with time. No wonder, a question that we all feel tempted to ask is whether it is possible to be free from work. There are moments when we ask this question out of our *tamasic* tendencies—out of passivity, inertia, laziness, dullness. Again, there are occasions when we ask this question because of boredom, the meaninglessness we find in our work. Furthermore, we ask this question out of our aspiration for a utopia: a world in which everything is being done by the machine. After all, amongst us there are great believers in technology—its ability to perform miracles, and make us free from toil and labour. In that utopia, it is believed, there is only leisure and play; and we all eat, drink, sleep, love, play and dance! This is not the only story. We often lament, we complain that while we are working day and night, someone else is lucky because he does not have much work to do. And hence a civil servant complains: 'My work does not stop. But see this university professor. He is enjoying his life. He delivers just one lecture, and enjoys his coffee! ' Or a tired/defeated lower middle class salesperson laments: 'See this politician. He has earned so much that his children and grandchildren can live happily without doing any work.' In other words, there are moments when, it seems, we are ambiguously engaged with work; we work; yet, we strive for a situation in which there is no work.

However, we have been reminded: 'Don't fear work. Don't escape it. Everyone ought to work.' Even the meaning of renunciation, we are told, has to be understood properly; it should not be seen as an escape from the world, its activities. It should not mean a retreat, a flight into another world. At this juncture, it is great to recall Krishna, and his assertive declaration in the *Bhagavad Gita*: 'There is not for me, O Partha, any work in the three worlds which has to be done, nor anything to be obtained; yet I am engaged in work.' (III: 22). Yes, Krishna is the embodiment of the all-pervading Energy. He is Infinite. As it is believed, 'Of the great sages he is Bhrgu, of utterances, he is the syllable Aum; of offerings he is the offering of silent meditation, and of immovable things he is the Himalaya; of creations he is the beginning, the end and also the middle; of the sciences he is the science of the self; he is death, the all-devouring; he is the origin of things that are yet to be; of the deceitful he is the gambling; of the splendid he is the splendour; he is victory, he is effort and he is the goodness of the good; he is the seed of all existences; there is nothing that can exist without him' (X: 25, 32, 34, 36, 39). Although there is no end to his divine manifestations, Krishna is here amongst us, he is working, he is in the battlefield, he is counselling Arjuna, and he makes it clear: 'Works do not defile Me; nor do I have yearning for their fruit. He who knows Me is thus not bound by work' (IV: 14). And the *Bhagavad Gita*, as a result, gives us a remarkably penetrating insight into the philosophy of work.

Work becomes bondage when our egos get involved, when the calculative logic of personal gain/loss becomes important; and then work leads to stress, jealousy, fear, and everything because of mad attachment to our egos and fruits of action; but when work is an offering, an act of prayer, a piece of *bhakti*, when work is not for any utilitarian interest, when work is an articulation of *dharma*, we become free. Work does not oppress us any more; nor does it alienate us. We work, we live in the world; yet, we are not affected by fear, anxiety and insecurity. The notion of renunciation that the *Bhagavad Gita* is teaching us takes us to the ideal of a *karmayogi*—one for whom work is a yoga, an experience of a merger of the finite and the infinite, the temporal and the transcendental. See the articulations of this ideal in the profoundness of Krishna's dialogue with Arjuna. True, no one can remain free even for a moment without doing work. But, Krishna reminds Arjuna, 'He who controls the senses by the mind, and without attachment engages the organs of action in the path of work, he is superior' (III: 7). And therefore, he can see inaction in action, action in inaction. Krishna adds, 'Having abandoned attachment to the fruit of works, ever content, without any kind of dependence, he does nothing though he is ever engaged in work' (IV: 20). A *karmayogi* of this kind is 'satisfied with whatever comes by chance'; he has passed beyond 'the dualities of pleasure and pain'; he remains the same in 'success and failure'; no wonder, 'even when he acts, he is not bound' (IV: 22).

It is indeed a difficult ideal. One may feel tempted to say that here is an impossible project. How can we work without any expectation, without bothering about the fruits of action? Well, it is possible to imagine that the fruits I am expecting need not necessarily be for my selfish gains—wealth, fame, prosperity; but then, the expectation can be subtle and higher: say, making a difference in the life of others, bringing about peace, harmony, revolution, etc. In order to understand this complexity, let me reflect on my own vocation. I teach; I come to the classroom; I deliver a lecture. I like it; I am creatively involved in it. However, I am not indifferent to the fruits of my work. Whenever I come to the class, I come with a bundle of expectations: 'Let my lecture be understood; let my students find a meaning in what I am teaching; let them get inspired'. True, my expectations are not gross and crude. I am not demanding fame and money. Nevertheless, I am not free from desire. I desire something else: reciprocity from my students, their radiant smiles, their positive vibrations. And if I do not find it, I lose interest, I do not find sufficiently inspired to come to the class. What does the *Bhagavad Gita* say about this? Possibly it would remind me that I seem to have gone beyond the qualities of *tamas* and *rajas*, I have become somewhat *sattvic*. But my ego is still alive; I am attached to my ego—yes, a very subtle/refined ego. And 'it binds...by attachment to happiness and by attachment to knowledge' (XIV: 6). Even this attachment, as far as this profound ideal is concerned, must go; yet, I should be able to teach with all zeal and intensity, improve my teaching; but this very act ought to be realized as an offering, a service, a flow of energy that just happens to radiate through my embodied existence. I should be free from the notion that 'I am the doer'. In other words, I should be free from not only *tamas* and *rajas*, but also from *sattva*. Is it possible? It baffles even Arjuna. He asks: 'By what marks is he, O Lord, who has risen above the three modes characterized? What is his way of life? How does he get beyond the three modes?' (XIV: 21) And see the amazing reply Krishna gives: 'He who regards pain and pleasure alike, who dwells in his own self, who looks upon a clod, a stone, a piece of gold as of equal worth, who remains the same amidst the pleasant and unpleasant things, who is of firm mind, who regards both blame and praise as one' (XIV: 24).

Yes, I see its appeal. It is like becoming a flower radiating its beauty without bothering whether others are noticing it, appreciating it. The *swadharma* of a flower is to radiate its fragrance; the *swadharma* of a teacher is to teach and bloom like a flower; nothing else matters. Difficult; yet, immensely magical and appealing!

The debate does not end here. One might ask a question: Isn't it a fact that this very *swadharma* (with its principle of detached work) is misleading, a device to hide oppression and injustice? Imagine, for instance, a wage earner in a factory working day and night, and getting exploited. Is it desirable on his part to give his consent to Krishna's advice: 'Better is one's own law though imperfectly carried out than the law of another carried out perfectly. Better is death in the fulfilment of one's own law, for to follow another's law is perilous' (III: 35)? Should he continue to work without expecting better wages, better living conditions, better working environment? It is here, as we know, that the experience of *alienation* becomes significant. It was Karl Marx who spoke—and spoke with great passion—about alienation: how, say, in a class-divided/ private-property oriented/ capitalist economy workers get alienated from their work, because the very nature of work is utterly mechanical and fragmented. Because 'the object which labour produces...confronts it as something alien, as a power independent of the producer' (Marx 1977: 68). Under these circumstances, 'labour appears as loss of realization for the workers' (Ibid: 68). The worker does not have any control over what he produces. Even though 'labour produces wonderful things for the rich', as Marx wrote, 'for the worker it produces privation; it produces palaces—but for the worker, hovels; it produces beauty—but for the worker, deformity; it produces intelligence—but for the worker, stupidity, cretinism' (Ibid: 70). This is alienation. In his work the worker 'does not affirm himself but denies himself, does not feel content but unhappy, does not develop freely his physical and mental energy but mortifies his body and ruins his mind' (Ibid: 71). Alienation means that labour is not voluntary; it is forced; and 'as soon as no physical or other compulsion exists, labour is shunned like the plague' (Ibid: 71). Can such a worker afford to experience his work as an offering, a manifestation of love, creativity and *bhakti*? Certainly not. And I would imagine that even a meaningful engagement with the *Bhagavad Gita* would lead to the same conclusion. After all, the battelefield of Kurukshetra is an important metaphor; it is for justice; it is for the restoration of good over evil. 'Whenever there is a decline of righteousness and rise of unrighteousness', Krishna reminds Arjuna, 'I send forth Myself' (IV: 7). Because, as Krishna declares, 'for the protection of the good, for the destruction of the wicked and for the establishment of the righteousness, I come into being from age to age' (IV: 8). And hence a battle ought to be fought against exploitation. That, I believe, is the true *swadharma* of a worker, provided, instead of a superficial reading of the *Bhagavad Gita*, we understand its deeper symbolic meaning. A worker should fight this battle not because he wishes to become like a capitalist, and enjoy the privileges he is deprived of. Instead, he ought to fight this battle for truth, for justice, for creating a world free from exploitation, a world in which, to borrow Marx's prophetic words, 'there is a genuine resolution of the conflict between...man and man—the true resolution between objectification and self-confirmation, between freedom and necessity, between the individual and the species' (Marx 1977: 97). In a way, in this struggle, or in his *swadharma* he would transcend himself—his limited self, his own misery and gain, and merge himself with a deeper ideal. His struggle itself becomes an act of prayer, an offering; it becomes more than merely a temporal/calculative logic of trade unionism. This is what I wish to regard as the poetry of protest—something that the political class needs to engage with.

Possibly with all these deliberations we are reflecting on the moot question: How can our work make us free? How can it become a kind of yoga through which we overcome our limitedness, and become an integral part of the flow of universal energy? This, it may be argued, is difficult, apparently impossible. For the alienated man, it is not easy to even imagine such a possibility. As Marx said with deep pain, 'the care-burdened, poverty-stricken man has no sense for the finest play; the dealer in minerals sees only the commercial value but not the beauty and the specific character of the mineral: he has no mineralogical sense' (Ibid: 103). Moreover, because of a minute form of division of labour in a modern/technological society we are becoming increasingly fragmented, mechanical and insulated. We work, we draw our salary, we retain a standard of living; but we remain disconnected from the whole—the rhythm of connectedness. Imagine that you are a cashier in a bank; from 9 am to 5 pm you are counting money, you are keeping the records; and when the bank closes you are tired, exhausted; you take your drink, watch TV serials, eat, sleep; and again the next morning you start the same process... Or imagine you are a management executive in a liquor company; your boss has given you the target, you spend sleepless nights, and all the time you think of how to promote the sale of liquor. And one day you realize that for years you have not looked at the sky, you have forgotten the beauty of sunrise and sunset; you have not read the poem you always wanted to read; and you have failed to notice the mystery in your wife's eyes. Yet, you carry on; the lure of money, the fear of losing the job, the fear of the boss, the desire for yet another promotion—there is no end to justification; but from deep inside every day you get wounded. Or imagine the kind of work that is being performed as a kind of what Erving Goffman would regard as 'impression management' (Goffman 1959). The sphere of work is a 'front stage'; one is playing a role—a sort of theatrical performance, and trying to impress the audience. Imagine a waiter in a restaurant, or a glamorous air hostess in an airplane—it is like playing a 'role' with its carefully designed script; in a work of this kind one is not oneself; one is, to use the existentialist vocabulary, 'inauthentic'. If you look at the air hostess carefully, you will not fail to notice tiredness and deep pain beneath her decorated body and synthetic smile. Indeed, from Marx's 'estranged/alienated' labour to a young girl in a call centre, from a railway booking clerk to a management professional in a transnational company, from a waiter in a restaurant to a glamorous air hostess—the experience is certainly not what Schumacher would have regarded as 'good work': the kind of work through which one realizes one's innate possibilities, one relates to others, contributes to our collective happiness, and one liberates oneself from one's 'inborn egocentricity' (Schumacher 1980). Not solely that. Our survival anxiety, our fear and insecurity, our attachment to fame and glamour, and our boredom and poverty of imagination make us wounded and crippled. So where is the scope for work becoming a kind of yoga, meditation, a creative accomplishment?

Yet, as I insist, it is this longing that makes us special. And even when we are under the most difficult circumstances, we should not forget our possibilities, our prayer. That is why, the *Bhagavad Gita* is so inspiring. A discourse on yoga in the battlefield—what else could be more inspiring? It is equally promising to come across Marx's grand optimism: 'Man produces even when he is free from physical need and only truly produces in freedom therefrom. Man therefore also forms objects in accordance with the laws of beauty' (Ibid: 74).

What does one do? For most of us creative work does not exist because the structural constraints of society and our own mental structure are not yet conducive to it. But then, we must strive for good work, because striving for good work is like striving for a good world; it is a process, it is a struggle, and like all great struggles, it is an act of prayer. Striving for good work is also like choosing one's priorities—inner fulfilment or outer glamour; and above all, it is also for evolving a domain of possibilities even in a difficult situation. And only then can we find light amidst darkness, creativity in an otherwise alienated world, a fountain in a desert, and Arjuna listening to Krishna. That is why, it is nice to come across—yes, even in these difficult times—an accountant in an LIC office radiating positive vibrations, talking gently with every customer, and evolving a bond with them. It is great to find a security guard showing great reverence to all elderly women in the street, and working with joy and alertness. Here work becomes more than just a paid job; work becomes greater than just one's technically defined official duty; here work is an opportunity to relate to others, to realize one's positivity; work becomes musical and relational. That is why, I have always believed that creativity is not something that is limited to a select few: musicians, poets, artists, scientists. Each of us is potentially creative. Creativity is not what we do; creativity is how we do it. A professor can be non-creative; a housewife can be creative. A corporate executive can be non-creative; a simple gardener can surprise you with his creativity. Creativity is like doing things with joy and wonder; creativity is like making a difference in the routine of everydayness, and transforming the mundane into the sacred; creativity is like establishing a communion with one's inner self and the world; creativity is relatedness. Yes, there are constraints and obstacles—from the burden of 'ego' to the logic of domination implicit in a divided society. Yet, creativity in what we do, or work as an affirmation of love is our ultimate quest; it is our potential. And what is the meaning of our wealth, technology, industry and market if this potential does not unfold itself, if we continue to miss creativity and music in life?

## (II)

Our orientation to life-affirming/meaningful work leads us to our quest for a good society. A good society is one in which work is creative, life is relational, and responsibility emanates from a sense of freedom. But the question is what sort of a society we actually live in. We often express our anguish and discomfort—the society we live in is conflict-ridden; it is full of violence and exploitation; it is a domain of inequality; it does not enable most of us to experience creative freedom or love in our domains of work. And while looking at this discord we tend to reflect on *power*, its unevenness, its aberrations, its constraining features. Power divides and hierarchizes; power restrains; power leads to conflict; and politics, we all know, is centred on power—its possession and distribution. True, at an elementary level, power is the ability to do things; it is the ability to work. It is in this sense that we realize the power of intelligence, the power of physical/mental strength. And we all strive for this kind of power. But then, power is not just one's ability to do things; it also reveals the nature of one's engagement with others; power is embedded in a network of social relationships; power, as it is exercised by some, makes others powerless. 'Power', wrote Max Weber, 'is the probability that one actor within a social relationship will be in a position to carry out his own will despite resistance, regardless of the basis on which this probability rests' (Weber in Parsons 1964: 152). We find ourselves in a society in which, for instance, cops have got the power over those who deviate from established rules; parliamentarians have got the power to legislate, and teachers have got the power to take exams, and evaluate their students. This sort of power, as Weber would have said, is 'legitimate'. Cops have power because they represent the 'legitimate' authority of the state; or parliamentarians have power because parliament is a body legitimated by the Constitution. Legitimate power, for Weber, is 'authority'; and it is different from, say, illegitimate power—the power that a man exercises over a woman while violating her dignity, or the power of brute force that a robber exercises over his victim. To put it otherwise, what signifies legitimate power or authority is that it increases the probability that 'certain commands (or all commands) from a given source will be obeyed by a given group of persons' (Ibid: 324). Or, a criterion of every true relation of legitimate authority is 'a certain minimum of voluntary submission' (Ibid: 324).We know that Weber talked about three pure types of legitimate authority. To begin with, 'traditional authority' rests on an established belief in 'the sanctity of immemorial traditions and the legitimacy of those exercising authority under them'; 'charismatic authority' rests on 'devotion to the specific and exceptional sanctity, heroism or exemplary character of an individual person'; and finally, 'legal authority' rests on a belief in the 'legality' of patterns of normative rules and the right of those elevated to authority under such rules to issue commands' (Ibid: 328). Living in human society is like experiencing all these types of authority—say, the traditional authority of a father, the charismatic authority of a prophet or a saint, and the legal authority of a civil servant. What, however, distinguished Weber was his firm conviction that modernity could not be understood without the assertion of 'legal authority with a bureaucratic administrative staff'. All modern institutions—banks, financial corporations, industries, universities, it is believed, are governed by bureaucracy. Capitalism, according to Weber, has played a major role in the development of bureaucracy. The very rationale of capitalistic production seems to have created an urgent need for 'stable, strict, intensive, and calculable administration'; and it is this need which gives bureaucracy 'a crucial role in our society as the central element in any kind of large-scale administration' (Ibid: 338). For Weber, even socialism would not be able to alter this fact. In fact, it might require 'a still higher degree of formal bureaucratization than capitalism' (Ibid: 339).

How does bureaucracy as a network of power relations function, and affect our everyday existence? Let us gain some insights from the Weberian *ideal type* of bureaucracy. It rests on a consistent system of 'abstract rules'; the typical person in authority occupies an 'office', and 'in the action associated with his status, including the commands he issues to others, he is subject to an impersonal order to which his actions are oriented' (Ibid: 330); the organization of offices follows the 'principle of hierarchy'; each lower office is under the control and supervision of a higher one; administrative acts, decisions and rules are 'formulated and recorded in writing'. Its implications are clear. It means 'the dominance of a spirit of formalistic impersonality...without hatred or passion, and hence without affection or enthusiasm'; and 'everyone is subject to formal equality of treatment' (Ibid: 340). Yes, bureaucracy, it can be argued, has its positive functions; it reduces the possibility of arbitrariness; it tends to eliminate class privileges because 'it places everyone in the same empirical situation'; indeed, 'every process of social levelling creates a favourable situation for the development of bureaucracy' (Ibid: 340). But then, it should not be forgotten that bureaucracy dehumanizes; rules become abstract and impersonal; rules become overwhelmingly powerful over the concreteness of the human condition; we lose our humanness; we get caught into a complex chain of written documents and official files. No wonder, bureaucracy loses imagination and creativity; even a top bureaucrat feels helpless before the rules that govern his activities. A typical bureaucrat is the embodiment of an alienated self; he cannot feel, he cannot listen to his inner voice, he cannot do anything even if his conscience goes against those abstract rules. We feel lost before the anonymity of bureaucracy—its abstraction and formalism; it is like confronting a huge machine on which we have no control. It is an experience of utter helplessness. In order to articulate the intensity of this pathos, I feel like referring to Franz Kafka's immensely penetrating novel *The Trial* (Kafka 1982). Look at the fate of Joseph K.—a Bank official. One fine morning he finds himself arrested. He does not know the reason; nobody can specify the charge against him. Kafka depicts these perplexing experiences Joseph K. passes through. He thinks he is innocent. This sudden arrest makes him wonder; he wants to know the reason. But then, at the very beginning the Inspector tells him: 'I can't even confirm that you are charged with an offence, or rather I don't know whether you are. You are under arrest, certainly, more than that I do not know' (Ibid: 18). Moreover, he is told that although he is under arrest, he won't be hampered in carrying on in the ordinary course of his life. As the novel progresses, we see how Joseph K. finds himself in a world in which every encounter intensifies his worry, and makes him feel that while everybody he meets knows about his case, he himself does not know what it is all about; there is no clarity; mysteries surround his existence. It is true that at the beginning he does not lose his nerve. In fact, at the time of the first interrogation he is bold in asserting: 'There can be no doubt that behind all the actions of this court of justice, there is a great organization at work. An organization which not only employs corrupt warders, stupid Inspectors, and Examining Magistrates, but also has at its disposal a judicial hierarchy of high, indeed of the lowest rank, with an indispensable and numerous retinue of servants, clerks, police, and other assistants, perhaps even hangmen...And the significance of this great organization, gentlemen? It consists in this, that innocent persons are accused of guilt, and senseless proceedings are put in motion against them, mostly without effect, it is true, as in my own case' (Ibid: 54-55). Yet, things are not easy. He begins to realize how helpless he is; the entire world confronts him as a conspirator; it stigmatizes him; it advises him; but the truth continues to hide itself. His uncle arrives; he shows his concern; he takes him to an advocate who happens to be his friend. And with utter surprise K. comes to know that the advocate is already familiar with his case. What the advocate says is bound to puzzle him: 'I'm an advocate, you see, I move in circles where all the various cases are discussed, and the more striking ones are bound to stick in my mind, especially the one that concerns the nephew of an old friend of mine. Surely that's not so extraordinary' (Ibid: 115). There seems to be no end to this bewilderment. K. happens to meet a manufacturer in his Bank, and even he knows about it. 'You are involved in a case, aren't you?' he asked. Not solely that, he advises K. to meet a painter called Titorelli from whom he has heard of his case. 'So many people seem to be connected with the Court! ' said K. with a bowed head (Ibid: 150). He is told that Titorelli works for the Court; he draws portraits of the Judges; and it is possible for him to use his contacts and help him. Eventually, K. meets the painter. He speaks of three possibilities—definite acquittal, ostensible acquittal, and indefinite postponement. The complexity of the entire discourse confuses and puzzles him; he seeks to escape. But can he escape at all? He realizes that the Law-Court offices are everywhere; he is under constant observation; he cannot escape the gaze. Meanwhile, an Italian colleague has arrived. The Bank has given him the responsibility to show him the Cathedral in the town. See his destiny. The Court seems to have followed him even in the Cathedral. The priest identifies him. 'You are an accused man', said the priest in a very low voice. 'Yes', said K., 'so I have been informed'. 'Then you are the man I seek', said the priest. 'I am the prison chaplain' (Ibid: 231-32). He tells him a story—a metaphorical story that indicates the inevitable fate of Joseph K., and frightens him further. As the story goes, before the Law stands a doorkeeper on guard. 'To this doorkeeper comes a man from the country who begs for admittance to the Law. But the doorkeeper says that he cannot admit the man at the moment...There he sits waiting for days and years. He makes many attempts to be allowed in and wearies the doorkeeper with his importunity. The doorkeeper often engages him in brief conversation, asking him about his home and about other matters, but the questions are put quite impersonally, as great men put questions, and always conclude with the statement that the man cannot be allowed to enter yet...Finally, his eyes grow dim and he does not know whether the world is really darkening around him or whether his eyes are only deceiving him...The doorkeeper perceives that the man is at the end of his strength and his hearing is failing, so he bellows in his ear: 'No one but you could gain admittance through this door, since this door was intended only for you. I am now going to shut it' (Ibid: 236-37). Kafka takes us to the end. Everything around him seems to be inexplicable; there is no clarity or reason anywhere.The officials (or, murderers) are about to kill Joseph K., and at that very moment something happens. It seems he is seeing a human figure stretching both his arms. Is it a ray of hope? 'Who was it? A friend? A good man? Someone who sympathized? Someone who wanted to help? Was it one person only? Or were they all there? Was help at hand? Were there some arguments that had been overlooked? Where was the Judge whom he had never seen? Where was the High Court to which he had never penetrated? He raised his hands and spread out all his fingers' (Ibid: 250-51). Yes, they have already thrust the knife into his heart and turned it there twice. With failing eyes K. could still see two of them watching the final act. 'Like a dog! ' he said: it was as if he meant the shame of it to outlive him' (Ibid: 251).

Weber too could see the discontents of bureaucracy—how its 'iron cage' leads to helplessness. Who else is Joseph K. except a tragic victim of this 'iron cage'? Yes, power alienates; power brutalizes. But then, power, it may be said, is everywhere, not just in the bureaucracy. Power is in the family, in the prison, in the hospital, in the school. Parents have power over the child; wardens, councillors, psychiatrists , judges have power over the prisoners; doctors and nurses have power over the patients; and teachers have power over their students. In other words, power is not just the power of the state: the bureaucracy or the judiciary; power is not just the power of the dominant class—the bourgeoisie over the proletariat. Beyond this macro domain lies, said Michel Foucault, the 'micro- physics of power'. And this power, added Foucault, is not separated from knowledge. Power produces knowledge; knowledge produces power. Because 'there is no power relation without the correlative constitution of a field of knowledge, nor any knowledge that does not presuppose and constitute at the same time power relations' (Foucault 1979: 27). Power is deeply related to discourses on 'normalcy', 'mental health', 'sexsuality'. No wonder, power disciplines, hierarchizes and normalizes; power leads to surveillance. Foucault showed how the medieval penal theory and practice gave way in France, after the Revolution, to an institutionalization of imprisonment based on quite different theoretical premises.

In the new prison physical pain was no longer a necessary element in punishment. The body was touched as little as possible; instead, the expiation that was once inflicted on the body must be replaced by a punishment that acts in depth on the heart, the mind, the will. A whole army of technicians—wardens, doctors, psychiatrists, psychologists, educationalists—took over from the executioner; and they reassure it that 'the body and pain are not the ultimate objects of its punitive action' (Ibid: 11). That is why, as Foucault made a penetrating observation, 'today a doctor must watch over those condemned to death, right up to the last moment—thus juxtaposing himself as the agent of welfare, as the alleviator of pain, with the official whose task it is to end life' (Ibid: 11). In other words, the exercise of power, far from being violent, became a 'calculated, organized, technically thought out' exercise of discipline. These techniques of discipline and observation were not limited to the new prison. As Foucault demonstrated, there was an astonishing coincidence between the new prison and other contemporary institutions: hospital, factory, school, and barracks. In fact, Jeremy Bentham's famous 'panopticon'—a circular building enclosing a central inspection tower—was recommended for all these institutions. Foucault wrote in details about the exercise of power: how 'discipline increases the forces of the body (in economic terms of utility), and diminishes these same forces (in political terms of obedience)'; how discipline 'turns the body into an aptitude, a capacity which it seeks to increase', but at the same time, how 'it reverses the course of the energy, the power that might result from it, and turns it into a relation of strict subjection' (Ibid: 138). And we come to know how these techniques of discipline are rooted in all these 'carceral' institutions. Discipline requires the distribution of individuals in space; it requires 'enclosure' because the aim is 'to know where and how to locate individuals, to set up useful communications, to be able at each moment to supervise the conduct of each individual, to assess it, to judge it, to calculate its qualities or merits' (Ibid: 143). Discipline requires the time-table; it establishes rhythms, regulates the cycles of repetition, and controls one's activity. Discipline requires 'exercise' because it is a technique by which 'one imposes on the body tasks that are both repetitive and different, but always graduated' (Ibid: 161). Discipline requires 'hierarchical observation' because 'the perfect disciplinary apparatus would make it possible for a single gaze to see everything constantly' (Ibid: 173). Discipline requires 'normalizing judgement' because 'it differentiates individuals from one another, in terms of the following overall rule', because 'it measures in quantitative terms and hierarchizes in terms of value the abilities, the level, the nature of individuals', because 'it differentiates, hierarchizes, homogenizes, excludes and *normalizes*' (Ibid: 183). And discipline requires 'examination' because 'it places individuals in a field of surveillance, situates them in a network of writing, and engages them in a whole mass of documents that capture and fix them' (Ibid: 189).

As a matter of fact, for Foucault, power—with all its techniques of discipline and surveillance—is all-pervading. We experience it when schools (through weekly tests, parent-teacher meetings, assemblies, awards, prizes and ranking) 'normalize' us, educate us, and certify our merit and intelligence. We experience it when doctors and psychiatrists (through regular tests, observation and counselling) seek to make us follow the discourse of reason and perfect health. And we experience it when the CCTV camera observes us at railway stations, airports and market places, when every aspect of our existence is documented and recorded. Indeed, we are in the society of 'the teacher-judge, the doctor-judge, the social worker-judge'; and it seems that 'it is on them that the universal reign of the normative is based'; and, as Foucault wrote with great sharpness, 'each individual, wherever he may find himself, subjects to it his body, his gestures, his behaviour, his aptitudes, his achievements' (Ibid: 304).

From the 'iron cage' of bureaucracy to the cycle of 'micro-physics of power'—there seems to be no escape. Power observes; power controls; power restrains. But then, is power necessarily bad? Yes, at one level, as we have already said, the asymmetrical distribution of power leads to alienation and helplessness and negation of creativity in work; and, as Foucault said, it indicates a 'military dream of society', its reference is to the 'meticulously subordinated cogs of a machine', it refers to 'automatic docility' (Ibid: 169). Yet, at another level, power does things, power makes the machine run, power produces knowledge. Moreover, we all appreciate some sort of power—the power of knowledge and intelligence, the power of wisdom and character. It is in this sense that we love the power of a teacher—the power to teach, and inspire her students; we adore the power of a doctor—the power to heal, and generate hope in the mind of the patient; we admire the power of a civil servant—the power to fight corruption, and implement the welfare policies of the state. However, we loathe the abuse of power: when power humiliates us, subjugates us, negates our dignity, our spirit, our conscience. Hence we loathe the power of a cop who, in the name of retaining 'order', misuses his uniform, and insults people; we loathe the power of a doctor when he objectifies the patient, becomes non-transparent, and refuses to engage with his living spirit; we loathe the power of a teacher when discipline degenerates into corporal punishment; and we loathe the power of a father when his patriarchal ego gets inflated, and he refuses to listen to his wife and children. Or, while many of us would love to be touched by the power of a Gandhi or a Mother Teresa, we get horrified if we see the arrival of a Hitler or a Mussolini in our society. Not surprisingly, power becomes a major issue of contestation in society. In fact, politics is centred on power—its location and its dissemination, its control and its distribution, its management and its uses.

Is it possible to have a political vision that can fight the brutality of power, its asymmetrical distribution, and take us towards a new society in which we all have power; and power, instead of constraining and suppressing others, enables each of us to evolve and grow, find our vocation, and unfold our potential? Weber, it seems, was not so optimistic; for him, it was not so easy to transcend the 'iron cage' of bureaucracy, and resultant 'disenchantment'. And even Foucault would not allow us to believe that there could be a grand/universal project of freedom, and one day all the problems relating to the aberrations of power would be resolved. Because power relations 'go right down into the depths of society'; they are not situated 'in the relations between the state and its citizens or on the frontier between classes'; moreover, 'they are not univocal; they define innumerable points of confrontation and each of which has its own risks of conflict and struggles' (Ibid: 27). For Foucault, unlike the grand/meta theorists of emancipation, 'the overthrow of these micro-powers does not obey the law of all or nothing; it is not acquired once and for all by a new control of the apparatus nor by a new functioning or a destruction of the institutions' (Ibid: 27). Possibly there are innumerable narratives of local resistance and struggle.

However, no discussion on politics, power, and emancipation is complete without referring to Marx and Gandhi—their influence on people's quest for freedom. A look at the premises of historical materialism would suggest that, for Marx, the dominant class exercises power over the rest of society because they control the means of production, and because of its very location in the production process they are privileged to control the economy, the state, the political-cultural institutions. At times, the exercise of this power becomes visibly naked. This explains the brutality of a feudal landlord or a real estate mafia or a capitalist. From Kafka's Joseph K. to the agony of a landless peasant, from the murder of a committed trade union activist to the displacement of an *adivasi* from his land—we see how power coerces, and the story of subjugation and humiliation unfolds itself, and a meaningful life filled with freedom and creative work becomes an impossibility. And this asymmetry in power relations, and resultant conflict, violence and exploitation, according to the classical Marxian understanding, can be transcended only through a revolutionary practice: when the oppressed classes acquire their agency, mobilize themselves, become aware of their historic mission, refuse to be fooled by the ideological façade of the ruling class, overthrow the system, and lay the foundations of a new social order based on collective control over property. A scheme of this kind places extraordinary emphasis on the centrality of the economy, and radical politics, it is thought, must aim at overthrowing the capitalist state which is seen primarily as a coercive apparatus.

Antonio Gramsci—an Italian Marxist with his critique of positivism, vulgar evolutionism and determinism—gave a creative dimension to the understanding of the Marxian politics in our times. We are asked to rethink the character of the state in advanced capitalist countries. The state cannot be seen as just a coercive machine. After all, it should not be forgotten that 'the bourgeois class poses itself as an organism in continuous movement, capable of absorbing the entire society assimilating it to its own cultural and economic level'; and hence 'the entire function of the state has been transformed; the state has become an educator' (Gramsci 1971: 260). It is in this context that the notions of 'hegemony' and 'civil society' become relevant. Hegemony is not coercion; instead, it is a process through which 'the ruling class manages to win the active consent of those over whom it rules' (Ibid: 244). 'Every state', Gramsci reminded us, 'is ethical in as much as one of its most important functions is to raise the great mass of the population to a particular cultural and moral level, a level which corresponds to the needs of the productive forces for development, and hence to the interests of the ruling classes' (Ibid: 258). And this entire hegemonic function is being performed by civil society—'a multitude of private initiatives and practices'. As Gramsci would argue, in advanced capitalist countries, the general notion of the state ought to include elements which need to be referred back to the notion of civil society; in other words, 'state= political society+ civil society' (Ibid: 263). It is possible for the Marxists to debate whether in a country like ours the ruling class exercises its power through hegemony or through crude coercive practices and violence. It is quite likely that there is no single answer to this question, and power manifests itself in multiple ways. However, as I see, it is important to take Gramsci seriously, and appreciate the nuances in his argument.

Let us try to understand its implications with a simple illustration. The ruling class is powerful, and this power manifests itself in the visibility of 'success'; a member of the ruling class owns a factory, runs a newspaper, controls a television channel, buys a cricket team; and ordinary mortals seem terribly powerless before him because it is he who provides jobs, gives financial help to the political parties, and attends glamorous functions with the ministers, film stars, cricketers and media bosses. But then, he exercises this power not necessarily through the police and army; instead, quite often you and I give our consent to his power because we too have internalized the belief that 'nothing succeeds like success'; and this ideology enters our consciousness right from the day our schooling begins; schools make us believe in competitiveness, in the doctrine of the survival of the fittest, in hierarchy, in the difference between the privilege of 'success' and the stigma of 'failure'. The rulers have conquered our minds; we have internalized them; we wish to become like them. And hence if we want to alter this game of power it is not enough to alter the outer parameter of the state; what is equally important is to change our mindset, our belief system, our values and consciousness. In other words, a revolutionary struggle ought to be a struggle in the domain of culture, a struggle for fighting the existing hegemony, and creating a new one—particularly in a society in which civil society is deeply embedded.

'The superstructures of civil society', for Gramsci, 'are like the trench-systems of modern warfare' (Ibid: 235). The state is merely an outer ditch; and hence what is important is a continual ideological struggle for combating the old beliefs and diffusing a socialist 'counter-hegemony' among all potentially revolutionary subjects. This 'war of position' would become more and more significant with advancing stages of capitalist development, and this would prove to be the ultimate key to 'the war of movement'. In Russia, Gramsci kept reminding us, the state was everything, and 'civil society was primordial and gelatinous', but in the West 'there was a proper relation between state and civil society'; and behind the outer ditch of the state 'there stood a powerful system of fortresses and earthworks' (Ibid: 238). This means that in politics the 'war of position'is of great significance.

There is yet another important question that confronts us. Is it possible for a revolutionary struggle to remain free from the trap of asymmetrical power relations? It should not be forgotten that the leaders or the 'vanguard' often become overwhelmingly powerful; and, as history has demonstrated, the socialist state can degenerate into yet another form of authoritarianism. There was, however, a refreshing departure in Gramsci's agenda. He gave great importance to the role of 'organic intellectuals' in creating a counter-hegemony, and arousing the imagination of the masses. And these intellectuals should not be seen as insulated from the masses. Because it should not be forgotten that the masses too are potential intellectuals; 'each man...carries on some form of intellectual activity, that is, he is a philosopher, an artist, a man of taste'; in fact, 'there is no human activity from which every form of intellectual participation can be excluded: *homo faber* cannot be separated from *homo sapiens*' (Ibid: 9). This awakening generates humility, respect for the masses; and, therefore, there is no reason for these intellectuals to think that they are inherently superior, and they would only command and lead. As Gramsci said, 'the mode of being of the new intellectual can no longer consist in eloquence,...but in active participation in practical life, as constructor, organizer, permanent persuader...' (Ibid: 10). That is why, it is important to rethink the relationship between the intellectual activity and the muscular-nervous effort, and move towards a new equilibrium which ensures that 'the muscular-nervous effort itself, in so far as it is an element of a general practical activity ...becomes the foundation of a new and integral conception of the world' (Ibid: 9). To summarize, Antonio Gramsci (a modern karmayogi rethinking the philosophy of praxis in Mussolini's prison) pleaded for symmetry and dialogue in the relationship between the leaders and the led, labour and thought, work and creativity; and it is an important reminder because, without perpetual reflexivity, alertness and conscience, today's revolutionaries might become tomorrow's dictators!

It is at this juncture that I need to refer to Mohandas

Karamchand Gandhi. Gandhi, to use the Weberian category, possessed 'charismatic' authority; he was indeed immensely powerful. Yet, he was deeply aware of the aberrations of power; he wanted a society in which, instead of being ruled by others, we would be mature enough to govern our own destinies. 'It is swaraj when we learn to rule ourselves', said Gandhi. This meaning of swaraj makes us understand why he critiqued parliament, legal machinery or even modern medicine. All these institutions, for him, make us dependent, and generate passivity. For example, Gandhi did not hesitate to say that 'men become unmanly and cowardly when they resort to the courts of law', because 'the parties alone know who is right', but 'we, in our simplicity and ignorance, imagine that a stranger, by taking our money, gives us justice' (Gandhi 1989: 49). Or imagine a situation. You overeat; you have indigestion; you go to a doctor, and he gives you medicine. You are cured. However, you overeat again; you fall sick; you visit the doctor; and the cycle repeats itself. You lose control over your body, you become terribly dependent on modern medicine. Gandhi—with his characteristic simplicity and insight—would have advised you not to overeat because only then can you reduce your dependence on medicine. See the trap. In fact, the doctor 'intervened', and helped you to 'indulge' yourself. This leads to your helplessness because 'a continuance of a course of medicine must, therefore, result in loss of control over the mind' (Ibid: 51). If we lose this inner strength or 'soul-force' we lose our true independence; we then invent gigantic machines—a centralized state with its bureaucracy, an economy that sustains itself by stimulating our desire, or a huge techno-scientific enterprise that imposes itself on us, and get paralyzed by their demonic power. It should not be forgotten that when Gandhi was fighting colonialism, his goal was not just to replace one set of rulers by another because that would mean that 'we want the English rule without the Englishman' (Ibid: 26). He was striving for something deeper—a qualitative change in our thought, in our modes of living. The entire logic of colonial modernity, as Gandhi said repeatedly, is the negation of true religiosity, and 'it has taken such a hold on the people in Europe that those who are in it appear to be half mad' (Ibid: 33). Even though in a civilization of this kind 'people live in better-built houses than they did a hundred years ago', or instead of using their hands and feet, 'they press a button, and they have their clothing by their side', or 'they press another button, and they have their newspaper', Gandhi asked the colonized not to get seduced by it.'To what do you ascribe the state of England?'—the Reader asked the Editor in the *Hind Swaraj*; and the Editor replied: 'It is not due to any peculiar fault of the English people, but the condition is due to modern civilization. It is a civilization only in name. Under it the nations of Europe are becoming degraded and ruined day by day' (Ibid: 30). But then 'civilization is not an incurable disease'; and Gandhi's hope was that the real spirit of decolonization would enable both the colonizers and the colonized to heal themselves, and strive for a civilization based on 'good conduct'. We were told that 'the mind is a restless bird; the more it gets the more it wants, and still remains unsatisfied; the more we indulge our passions the more unbridled they become' (Ibid: 53). With this neurotic restlessness 'we become slaves and lose our moral fibre' (Ibid: 53). Not surprisingly then, for Gandhi, real swaraj or our freedom would mean a civilization based on massive decentralization (leading to 'oceanic circles'), people's resources, their 'soul-force', an economy organically related to environment, and above all, a mode of living that rests on the ethics of dharma, austerity and ahimsa. This is like seeing work as inspirational.

Power humiliates us, subjugates us, paralyzes us when we lose control over our destinies; when we get intoxicated, when we indulge ourselves, and become pathetically dependent on the ever-expanding needs. And power liberates us when we realize our own potential, when we acquire moral courage, when we resist temptation, overcome fear, and when we love. That is the journey—from Gramsci's 'war of position' to Gandhi's 'soul-force'. Power degenerates when it is based on 'brute-force'; it emancipates when it rests on 'soul-force'. 'Kings', wrote Gandhi, 'will always use their kingly weapons; to use force is bred on them' (Ibid: 72). But then, he wanted us to ask the moot question: 'Wherein is courage required—in blowing others to pieces from behind a canon, or with a smiling face to approach a canon and be blown to pieces? Who is the true warrior—he who keeps death always as a bosom friend, or he who controls the death of others' (Ibid: 70)? Gandhi's answer, we know, was clear. You are truly powerful and courageous when you rest your head upon death as its 'pillow' because 'those who defy death are free from all fear' (Ibid: 72). In other words, Gandhi gave us the strength to redefine power. Real power is not the power to dominate and exploit others, it is not arrogance; it is not brute-force; instead, real power is the courage to 'disregard unjust commands' without losing faith in 'soul-force'; real power is the power to 'follow truth, and cultivate fearlessness'; real power is the power to die, and hence the power to love.

In fact, without love, the exercise of power—even the power of the mother over the child, or the power of the doctor over the patient—becomes oppressive; it causes fear, suspicion, mistrust. But love unites and heals. It is like realizing that there is no greater power than love. Love conquers fear; love transcends dualism; love generates positive action, love transforms work into meditation. And love is also the power to surrender, the power to be reduced into zero, the power to be powerless. Or, to use Jalaluddin Rumi's prophetic language, 'through love, the dead man becomes alive; through love, the king becomes a slave'. In other words, love gives us that ultimate power— the power of not demonstrating, abusing it, the power to remain humble.

Can love or 'soul-force' be part of politics? Gandhi constructed his utopia on the basis of this hope. Politics, for him, ought to be seen as a spiritual quest—an attempt to eliminate 'brute-force', and cultivate 'soul-force'. Antonio Gramsci gave a nuanced cultural meaning to the struggle for socialism. And it can be said that Mohandas Karamchand Gandhi spiritualized the politics of socialism. 'Truth and ahimsa', he believed, 'must incarnate in socialism'. And 'this socialism is as pure as crystal'; it requires 'crystal-like' means to achieve it; we need to remember that 'the prince and the peasant will not be equalized by cutting off the prince's head' because 'one cannot reach truth by untruthfulness' (Gandhi in Murti 1970: 322). Gandhi was striving for 'truthful, non-violent and pure-hearted socialists'. Gandhi was striving for Karmayogis. When a teacher comes to the classroom, when a doctor touches the patient's body, when a civil servant talks to a villager—each of us ought to experience the touch of love because 'socialism begins with the first convert; and if there is one such, you can add zeros to the one and the first zero will account for ten and every addition will account for ten times the previous number' (Ibid: 322).

## (III)

Love can overcome the pathology of power; love can make work magical. But then, is it possible to love, to unite and relate, particularly when the society we live in is *stratified* and *hierarchical*, when it trains us to speak the language of separation and exclusion rather than communication and fusion? It is at this juncture that we are back to Karl Marx once again. Marx, we know, reminded us of the reality of 'class': how it divides, how it gives birth to a conflict-ridden society—the way 'freemen and slave, patrician and plebeian, lord and serf, guild-master and journeyman, in a word, oppressor and oppressed, stood in constant opposition to one another' (Marx and Engels 2012: 41). And a modern bourgeois society, as it is argued, is 'more and more splitting up into two great hostile camps, into two great classes directly facing each other: Bourgeoisie and Proletariat' (Ibid: 41). But then, what is 'class'? One's class position, for Marx, has to be understood in terms of one's engagement with the production process. Because, as it was articulated in *The German Ideology*, 'life involves before everything else eating and drinking, a habitation, clothing and many other things; the first historical act is thus the production of the means to satisfy these needs, the production of material life itself' (Marx and Engels 1976: 47). As a matter of fact, what individuals are 'coincides with their production, both with what they produce and with how they produce' (Ibid: 37). No wonder, the position which the individual occupies in the social organization of production is absolutely important in defining his life-project. He is directly interwoven with the material activity and the material intercourse of men—'the language of real life'. It indicates to which social class he belongs. In a capitalist society the bourgeoisie owns and controls the means of production; it has done away with the scattered state of the means of production; and, instead, it 'has centralized means of production, and has concentrated property in a few hands' (Marx and Engels 2012: 48).And the proletariat or the working class is a class of labourers 'who live only so long as they find work and who find work only so long as their labour increases capital' (Ibid: 51). They are mere wage earners, they sell their labour power for survival, they have no say in the production process, and 'like every other article of commerce they are exposed to all the vicissitudes of competition, to all the fluctuations of the market' (Ibid: 51). The relationship between these classes is bound to be conflict-ridden because there is conflict over the distribution of economic rewards. A question we come across in Marxist literature is whether wage-labour creates any property for the labourer. And we get the answer: 'Not a bit. It creates capital, i.e. that kind of property which exploits wage-labour, and which cannot increase except upon condition of begetting a new supply of wage-labour for fresh exploitation' (Ibid: 63). Furthermore, owing to the extensive use of machinery and to division of labour, the proletariat has become 'an appendage of the machine'. In fact, as Marx would argue, it is this awareness of the conflict of interests that would eventually lead the working class to get unified and become aware of its mission; or, to put it otherwise, it would lead to an important transformation: from a 'class in itself' to a 'class for itself'.

It has been argued that in the changing times the Marxian notion of class requires serious rethinking. First, in advanced capitalism, because of technology and 'knowledge economy', we see the proliferation of a new class consisting of professionals, technologists, managers and highly skilled personnel; this class cannot be fitted into the categories of 'bourgeoisie' and 'proletariat'. They are not like 'the lower middle class, the small manufacturer, the shopkeeper, the artisan, the peasant' who, as Marx and Engels felt, 'try to roll back the wheel of history' (Ibid: 57). Instead, as it is argued, they play an active role in the economy; their power and influence cannot be negated. Second, it can be argued that because of growing democratization and welfare policies pursued by the state, the kind of 'class conflict' that Marx imagined has ceased to exist.

These changes notwithstanding, what cannot be denied is the existence of classes. There may not be two central classes. We are living in a society characterized by multiplicity of classes—landless peasants, middle farmers, big landlords, capitalists, white collar professionals, lower middle class, poor workers in organized/unorganized sectors. The relationship among these classes may be more complex. However, one thing is certain. The relationship is not that of love and fusion. There are boundaries and walls erected by diverse (and at times, conflicting) conditions of life as defined by the economy. It is quite unlikely that the son of a white collar professional and the daughter of a landless peasant would study at the same school. Nor is it possible to imagine that a lower middle class primary school teacher can afford to buy the car that an industrialist gives to his daughter as a birthday gift. It is in this context that we need to recall Max Weber who too acknowledged the importance of classes as represented 'exclusively by economic interests in the possession of goods and opportunities for income' (Weber in Gerth and Mills 1946: 181). He could not deny that 'it is the most elemental economic fact that the way in which the disposition over material property is distributed among a plurality of people, meeting competitively in the market for the purpose of exchange, in itself creates specific life chances' (Ibid: 181). He further added that 'property' and 'lack of property' were the basic categories of all class situations. Let us understand it with a simple example. Suppose I am a high ranking executive in an industrial house. The fact that I have quite a high salary tends to shape my 'life chances'. I can buy an apartment in a fortified housing complex; I can change my old car and buy a new one; I can buy the best possible medical insurance; I can take my family to an esoteric place and enjoy my holidays. But suppose you are a lower division clerk in a government office. Your 'life chances' are likely to be different. Possibly you would rent a small house in the suburb of the city; you would travel in over-crowded buses; your children would go to poor quality government schools, and you would realize that five star super-speciality hospitals do not exist for your kind of people. In other words, you and I live in two different worlds; and it is not easy for these two worlds to meet.

Doubtless, class positions and relations are important. But then, as Weber reminded us, 'status' is no less important in stratifying our society. 'In contrast to the purely economically determined class situation', wrote Weber, 'we wish to designate as 'status situation' every typical component of the life fate of men that is determined by a specific, positive or negative, social estimation of *honour*' (Ibid: 187). It is, of course, true that one's class position may shape one's honour; yet, it should be remembered that one's 'status honour' may not be entirely determined by one's class or economic position. For example, a great literary figure, or an eminent artist may have higher honour or status than, say, a wealthy real estate business man. One with a higher 'status honour' has a special 'style of life'. That is why, an artist or a novelist may be seen to be interested in the music of Mozart and Ravi Shankar, the cinema of Chaplin and Ray, or specific handloom wears; whereas a rich real estate business man, despite his wealth, may not be able to appreciate all this, even if he pretends to do so. It is, therefore, not surprising that 'all groups having interests in the status order react with special sharpness precisely against the pretensions of purely economic acquisition' (Ibid: 192). Indeed, 'status honour is normally expressed by the fact that above all else a specific *style of life* can be expected from all those who wish to belong to the circle' (Ibid: 187). It is this style of life that brings everyone belonging to the circle together; they feel comfortable in each other's company; they share their music, culinary practices, artistic possessions; in a way, as Weber observed, '*status groups* are normally communities' (Ibid: 186). If 'class' divides us in terms of wealth, 'status' divides us in terms of 'honour' and 'prestige'. You are a professor of literature in a reputed university. You love to read Amitav Ghosh and Salman Rushdie. You watch select Iranian and French films at film festivals. You have your own circle of friends—a civil servant who was your classmate in your college, a theatre personality, a civil rights activist, a feminist theorist—with whom you meet at the India International Centre. But I am a bank employee. Whenever I get time, I love to watch Amitabh Bachchan films. Beyond newspapers—I do not read much. Occasionally, I bring my family to India Gate, and enjoy *bhelpuri* and icecream. You dislike my taste; I find you snobbish. There is no bridge between us because 'status honour rests upon distance and exclusiveness'.

Possibly this entire Weberian insight can be compared with what Pierre Bourdieu is talking about in our times. One's 'cultural capital' leads to a 'sense of distinction'. It is a distinctive mark of one's personality; it is not just about one's economic capital (even though it may shape one's cultural capital); it is essentially about one's taste, one's choices, one's style, one's capacity to appreciate an 'object of quality'. For example, 'the objects endowed with the greatest distinctive powers are those which most clearly attest the quality of the appropriation, and therefore the quality of their owner, because their possession requires time and capacities which, like pictorial or musical culture, cannot be acquired in haste or by proxy, and which therefore appear as the surest indications of the quality of the person' (Bourdieu 1996: 281). Not surprisingly, Bourdieu would argue—particularly in the context of his own French society—that 'the purchase of works of art...is the distinctive signs and symbols of power' (Ibid: 282). See how a 'truly classical' university teacher, as Bourdieu gave an illuminating example, retains his cultural/symbolic capital, and distinguishes himself in terms of his taste. 'His reading is somewhat austere—no detective stories or novels. He has recently read *Deschooling Society* by Ivan Illich ('It made a great impression on me'), *Chance and Necessity* (Monod), and Konrad Lorenz's *On Aggression*. He owns a UNESCO *History of World Cultures* in seven or eight volumes....Something he browses in a great deal is the *Dictionary of Archaeology*' (Ibid: 289). Furthermore, for him, 'the summit of music is Mozart. He scarcely ever listens to light music or non-classical singers, and has never bought any of their records....He likes Truffaut but is impervious to the American arts. He would like to be able to play chess, and sometimes plays scrabble. He does a bit of photography. One thing he typically does when he is on holiday in the mountains is to take pictures of landscapes...then he spends hours poring over a map working out what can be seen' (Ibid: 290). Such distinctive cultural markers are bound to create islands of 'superiority' insulated from others.

What is clear is that a free/dialogic communication leading to a sense of togetherness and intimacy is not very easy in a stratified world. Instead, there are walls and boundaries; there is a logic of exclusion that separates 'people of our kind' from 'those who are not like us'. Hence we are so deeply bothered about our 'class', 'status honour', 'cultural capital', and our location in 'parties' which, as Weber added, 'live in a house of power', whose 'action is oriented towards the acquisition of social power, toward influencing a societal action' (Weber in Gerth and Mills 1946: 194).We are comparing, excluding, hierarchizing; we are by no means relating, uniting and loving.

As far as our own society is concerned, caste hierarchy has further complicated the situation. Enough has already been said and written about caste: how in terms of innumerable occupational groups caste or *jati* differs from the four-fold division of *varna*; how its *ascriptive* and *endogamous* character restricts mobility and communication; how the principle of *purity* and *pollution* legitimates hierarchy; how caste violence continues to prevail; how *Sanskritization*—the practice of emulation of 'forward caste' norms and life-practices by the 'lower' castes—further reinforces the hierarchical system; how the emergence of *dominant castes* adds yet another dimension (apart from the already existing ritualistic one) to the asymmetrical distribution of power; and how, despite modernity and liberal democracy, caste, far from withering away, assumes a political character, and becomes a source of mobilization and mobility. In other words, caste is in our consciousness. We speak of 'forward' castes and 'backward' castes; we speak of Brahmin votes and Dalit votes; in schools, universities and offices we cannot forget our caste identities because those identities matter. Caste is in census; caste is in marriage; caste is in application forms for jobs; caste is in elections. Caste, it seems, is all-pervading.

We all experience the implications of the caste system. We do realize that it is not just another form of division labour; nor is it a system based on symmetrical differences. True, 'hereditary specialization' as one of its central features may not exist in its pure form in our times. Not all Chamars, for instance, are tanners today; or, for that matter, even though the Baidyas in Bengal, according to their tradition, are a caste of doctors, many of them can be seen to be engaged in teaching, farming and business. We may find a Dalit Chief Minister, a Brahmin police constable, or a Rajput professor. However, despite this fluidity and changes, what cannot be denied is that caste is not dead; its spirit remains ruthlessly hierarchical; it degrades; it humiliates; it dehumanizes. 'When we say that the spirit of caste reigns in a society', C.Bougle observed with extraordinary sharpness, 'we mean that the different groups of which that society is composed, repel each other rather than attract, that each retires within itself, isolates itself, makes every effort to prevent its members from contracting alliances or even from entering into relations with neighbouring groups' (Bougle in Gupta 1994: 65). In other words, 'fear of impure contacts and repulsion from all those who are unrelated...are the characteristic signs of this spirit' (Ibid: 65).

We have not yet become free from this pathology. Caste prejudices and stereotypes, and terrible violence against the marginalized castes continue to characterize our society. Instead of giving yet another statistical document, I wish to refer to Munshi Premchand because literary creations reveal social reality more sharply and meaningfully than cold statistics. What he described in one of his illuminating short stories called *Salvation* (Premchand in Jalil 2011: 31-43) remains relevant even today. See its two central characters. Dukhi is a tanner. And Pandit Ghasiram is a Brahmin. Dukhi's daughter would be married; and hence he wanted to meet Pandit Ghasiram for fixing an auspicious occasion. Dukhi was waiting for him near the temple; and he 'jumped to his feet the instant he caught sight of Panditji, after prostrating before him, stood with folded hands and bowed head'. He appealed to Panditji to visit his house for fixing the date for his daughter's marriage. 'I have no time today, though I can drop by your house in the evening', said Panditji. Meanwhile, Dukhi was asked to chop a huge block of wood at Panditji's residence. Dukhi was hungry. He hadn't eaten a morsel for breakfast; there hadn't been a moment to spare in the morning. His own house was a mile away. If he went home for lunch, Panditji would get furious. And hence he smothered his hunger and set about chopping wood. It was an exceedingly difficult task. Dukhi was wielding the axe with all his might, but the axe would simply sheer off the block. 'Dukhi's body was bathed in sweat, his chest heaved and he slumped to the ground with exhaustion'. But then, he got up, and kept trying. 'His legs wobbled, his back ached, the world blurred before his eyes, his head swam and a strange, dizzy feeling overcame him.

Yet he went on doggedly lifting and striking the axe against the obstinate block of wood'.

Panditji had finished his meal; his wife thought of 'giving that tanner a bite to eat'. However, there were only a couple of rotis left over. But then, 'what good would two or three rotis be to him? He is a tanner and to him even a pound of flour would be a drop in the ocean'. So the idea of giving him some food was finally dropped. Dukhi kept working. It was 4 pm. Panditji had woken up, and he found the wood lying there, intact as before. He became furious. 'You can't chop a measly little piece of wood? Don't blame me if I don't stir myself to find a suitably auspicious occasion for your daughter's betrothal. It is no wonder that people say that when a low caste has enough to eat he will show his true colours'. Something happened to him. He lifted the axe yet again. The utter fatigue, hunger and tirednesss which had earlier overpowered him—all seemed to have disappeared quite miraculously. 'Like bolts of thunder, his axe fell on the block of wood. For a long time he went on attacking the wood in a paroxysm of maniacal energy till, finally, the wood split and the axe slipped from his hands. With that, he too fell to the ground. Driven by hunger, thirst and gut-wrenching fatigue, his weary body gave up'.

The news spread like wildfire in the village. It was a Brahmin village, and nobody would cross the road for fear of being defiled by mere sight of the tanner's corpse. No tanner came forward to carry the corpse away. The body began to stink. 'What else do you expect of a tanner's corpse? These people eat anything—clean or unclean'. Finally, Panditji got a rope, made a noose, pulled it through the dead man's feet and fastened it. He dragged the corpse and left it beyond the outskirts of the village. 'Then he came home, took a bath, read a passage from the scriptures and sprinkled the Ganga's holy water all over his home'. Yonder in the field, jackals and kites, dogs and crows were having a feast tearing away at Dukhi's body.

Is there anything more to be said? The fact is that all these hierarchical divisions block the free flow of communication. It negates love; it denies our egalitarian aspirations; it causes violence. But then, why do such divisions continue to exist? For a moment let us try to understand the arguments which are put forward for legitimizing this sort of stratification. It is indeed difficult to deny that our capacities, aptitudes, skills and orientations are different. For example, not everyone can prove to be a good mathematician or a good musician; or, for that matter, not everyone can be equally talented in sports, science and aesthetics. We need to acknowledge these differential aptitudes, and it is important that these special talents are encouraged and motivated with awards and prizes. Not to do so, as it would be argued, is to breed mediocrity and demotivate bright possibilities. It is thought that certain positions in any society are functionally more important than others, and require special skills for their performance, and only a limited number of individuals in any society have the talents which can be trained into the skills appropriate to these positions. Moreover, acquiring these skills involves a training period during which sacrifices of one kind or another are made by those undergoing the training. That is why, it is important to motivate these talented persons, and, as Kingsley Davis and Wilbert E. Moore asserted, 'a society must have, first, some kind of rewards that it can use as inducements, and, second, some way of distributing these rewards differentially to positions' (Davis and Moore in Bendix and Lipset 1966: 48). This means that 'social inequality is thus an unconsciously evolved device by which societies ensure that the most important positions are conscientiously filled by the most qualified persons' (Ibid: 48). Hence you should not complain if you find a doctor getting more reward (in terms of what Davis and Moore would love to characterize as 'sustenance and comfort', 'humour and diversion', and 'self-respect and ego expansion') than a nurse, or a nuclear physicist more privileged than his lab assistant. Even if you have a society in which there is equality of opportunity you cannot escape the fact that at the end of the day there are some who, precisely because of their talent and merit, would do better than others. And hence be prepared to accept the inevitability of social stratification!

This logic looks tempting. However, we should go deeper and explore alternative possibilities for restructuring our society—the way we look at ourselves and our relationships. It is of course true that in terms of capabilities and skills we are different. Someone is a doctor; someone is a nurse. Someone is an engineer; someone is a mechanic. But then, does it necessarily mean that there is no bridge between them? Or, does it necessarily imply that someone can be motivated to become a doctor or an engineer only if he/she is awarded with more money, more material comforts, more power? In a society that naturalizes inequality, competition and narcissism it may not be possible for us to think of any other possibility. But the challenge is to realize our innate potential which we may not be aware of. We have dissociated ourselves so much from this potential that we tend to think that it is merely an illusion, it does not exist. But nothing is finished for ever; we can keep it alive. It is in this context that I wish to argue that creative fulfilment and the willingness to serve may have more motivating power than money and comfort to inspire someone to undergo a rigorous process of training, acquire skills, and become a doctor or an engineer. To believe this is to realize and experience the power of love. An architect who constructs low cost houses for poor villagers earns less than one who works in a gorgeous real estate company. But then, the creative satisfaction that he gets, or people's faith and love that he receives is his ultimate award; it keeps him working. And it is this power of love that makes one see that, despite our differences in terms of occupational skills, there is something deep and profound that unites us. The affection that we see in a poor man's eyes when he embraces his little child is not different from that of a rich man; or, for that matter, all women, irrespective of their social ranking, trust their beloved in a similar way. Love, faith, trust, the innocence of an authentic smile, the depth of tears, the pain of separation, the ecstasy of the union between the lover and the beloved—all these experiences unite us, and remind us that it is the same Energy that passes through multiple forms, and true awakening is the awareness of this oneness (rather than being divided and fragmented in the name of economic/social/cultural capital). These are simple and eternal truths of human existence; but, because of our pride or wound relating to our class, caste and power, we have become incapable of living with these truths. Sociology can tell us about the entire science of this ignorance. But the task is to see beyond this science, overcome ignorance, and become awake, alive and deeply humane. Realizing this rhythm of connectedness, or this flow of love is like becoming humble; this is like refusing to claim excesses; this is like sharing, caring, distributing—not accumulating, possessing, exploiting. In this context it is indeed illuminating to recall a conversation between Jesus and a rich man who asked him: 'What must I do to inherit eternal life'? Jesus reminded him: 'Follow the commandments. Do not commit adultery, do not murder, do not steal, do not give false testimony, honour your father and mother'. 'All these I have kept since I was a boy', the rich man said. When Jesus heard this, he said to him: 'You still lack one thing. Sell everything you have and give to the poor, and you will have treasure in heaven. Then come, follow me'.

These days we use a different vocabulary—the language of social justice. However, we must ask the question: Is justice possible without inner awakening, without love, without the realization of our fundamental oneness? Is justice merely a question of legality, a constitutional provision, a service delivered by the bureaucratic machinery of the state? Yes, these are tools, important tools; but tools really work only when there is genuine concern. Without inner transformation, without the intensity of love, nothing actually works. You can have the Right To Education Act, but in the classroom you may find a teacher not very sensitive to the struggles and difficulties the child of a construction worker faces; or you may have strong constitutional provisions for the prevention of clild labour, but one day you may find yourself hiring a child for carrying your daughter's overloaded school bag. We all know and laugh at the gap between the legal provision and the actual practice. In other words, justice is not just a politico-legal question; it is fundamentally about love and conscience and inner transformation. If we look at the caste question in India, we can understand it much better.

Let us begin with Mohandas Karamchand Gandhi whose reading of the caste system was rather complex. In an article on Hinduism published in 1921, Gandhi called himself a 'sanatani Hindu', and declared his belief in the 'varnashrama dharma' in a 'strictly vedic sense', but not in its 'present popular and crude sense' (Gandhi in Murti 1970: 101). And hence for him, 'the four divisions define a man's calling; they define duties; they confer no privileges' (Ibid: 102). With his unique interpretative understanding he refused to accept that 'inter-dining or even inter-marriage necessarily deprives a man of the status that his birth has given him' because 'it is ...against the genius of Hinduism to arrogate to oneself a higher status or assign to another a lower' (Ibid: 102). Not surprisingly, while concluding the article Gandhi evolved a strong moral critique of the practice of untouchability which, for him, 'is repugnant to reason and to the instinct of mercy, pity or love' (Ibid: 105). The 'taint of untouchability' troubled him throughout his life. 'Let us not deny God', wrote Gandhi, 'by denying to a fifth of our race the right of association on an equal footing' (Ibid: 105). Gandhi seemed to be absolutely convinced of his moral position. In fact, in another article on the 'caste system' (published in 1920), he regarded untouchability as a 'heinous crime against humanity'; he would have no hesitation in rejecting 'scriptural authority of a doubtful character' because he would reject all authority 'if it is in conflict with sober reason or the dictates of the heart' (Ibid: 336). In fact, in yet another revealing piece (published in 1933), Gandhi regarded untouchability as 'the greatest blot on Hinduism'; and without moral and spiritual purification, as he felt, we would not be able to overcome it; 'the caste Hindus ...have to atone for the sin of untouchability' (Ibid: 357). That is why, he insisted, 'caste Hindus have to open their temples to Harijans, precisely on the same terms as the other Hindus'; it should not be forgotten that 'temple entry is the one spiritual act that would constitute the message of freedom to the untouchables and assure them that they are not outcastes before God' (Ibid: 357-58).

Indeed, for Gandhi, conscience or inner calling is absolutely important in any creative/constructive/radical endeavour. Gandhi could not be understood without his 'experiments'—without his authentic engagement with his own self. And from his innumerable experiments we come to know how he didn't allow the dogma of caste to affect his life-practice. It is in this context that I wish to refer to his rebellion against his caste association. Mohandas was young; and he decided to go to England for higher studies. However, his caste association was terribly against it because in the opinion of the caste, 'religion forbids voyages abroad; it is not possible to live there without compromising with one's religion; one is obliged to eat and drink with Europeans' (Gandhi 1976: 37). But he could manage to 'muster up courage' to protest. 'I do not think it is at all against our religion to go to England', replied young Mohandas. Needlessly to add, the caste association was deeply annoyed, and he was declared an 'outcaste'. It could not prevent him from going to England. That was Gandhi's spirit. His language was not possibly always very radical; but then, the life he led was always very revealing. Casteism and Gandhi—these were contradictory phenomena.

Take yet another illuminating experiment. Gandhi had finally arrived. From South Africa to India—a new journey; and he came to Risikesh, met many sadhus, and one of them was particularly attracted towards him. Gandhi had just returned from his bath in the Ganges; and this particular sadhu saw him 'bareheaded and shirtless'. As Gandhi described, the sadhu was 'pained to miss the *shikha* (tuft of hair) on my head and the sacred thread about my neck' (Ibid: 360). He was clear in his mind. The sacred thread, for him, should be 'a symbol of spiritual regeneration'; hence 'Hindus can vindicate the right to wear a symbol charged with such a meaning...only after Hinduism has purged itself of untouchability, has removed all distinctions of superiority and inferiority, and shed a host of other evils and shams that have become rampant in it' (Ibid: 361). The sadhu did not appreciate it; but Gandhi was Gandhi; he was clear in his conviction: 'When the symbol is made into a fetish and an instrument of proving one's superiority, it is fit only to be discarded' (Ibid: 361-62).

It was this emphasis on life-practice that distinguished Gandhi. For him, no radical change is possible without sharpening our moral sensibilities, our conscience, our everyday engagement with the world. However, B.R. Ambedkar—yet another important political figure—was not comfortable with Gandhi's approach to the caste question. Ambedkar was not in a mood to reform or humanize Hinduism. Instead, Hinduism, for him, is inherently hierarchical, its *dharmashastras* legitimate and sanctify caste hierarchy, and, therefore, without its abolition there is no freedom from casteism. And hence unlike Gandhi, Ambedkar evolved a sharp critique of the 'philosophy of Hinduism' itself. He took a hammer, and debunked the laws of Manu. Hinduism, as we were told, negates the principle of justice which is 'simply another name of liberty, equality and fraternity' (Ambedkar,Vol. 3 1987: 25). Take, for instance, liberty. Hinduism denies liberty because 'in the Scheme of Manu each man has his vocation preordained, and the occupation being preordained it has no relation to capacity nor to inclination' (Ibid: 39). Moreover, Hinduism compels people to serve ends chosen by others; it should not be forgotten that 'Manu tells the Shudra that he is born to serve the higher classes' (Ibid: 39). In other words, the Shudra, as Ambedkar would pinpoint, is a slave because 'a slave as defined by Plato means a person who accepts from another the purposes which control his conduct' (Ibid: 41). Again, liberty is impossible without the right to education; but then, Hinduism 'may be said to have been guilty for failing to take the responsibility for the education of the masses'; according to the law of Manu, 'reading and writing has become the right of the high class few and illiteracy has become the destiny of the low class many' (Ibid: 43).

Does Hinduism recognize equality? Ambedkar's answer was a clear 'no'. Here is a system in which 'the different castes are placed in a vertical series one above the other'; in fact, Manu 'made inequality the vital force of life' (Ibid: 25). Take, for instance, Rule of Law which is generally understood to mean equality before law. However, in Manu, as Ambedkar demonstrated, we find an 'irrational system of punishment'. Apart from the 'inhuman character of the punishment which has no proportion to the gravity of the punishment', the most striking feature of Manu's penal code 'which stands out in all its nakedness is the inequality of punishment for the same offence' (Ibid: 31). Likewise, the spirit of fraternity, said Ambedkar, is incompatible with the caste system. Fraternity means fellow feeling which leads an individual to identify himself with the good of others. But, as Ambedkar sought to remind us, there is no sharing among Hindus of joys and sorrows of life; the Hindu, it seems, is separate and exclusive all through his life. A foreigner coming to India, Ambedkar wrote with deep anguish, will find 'Brahmin Maternity Homes, Maratha Maternity Homes, and Bhatia Maternity Homes although Brahmins, Marathas and Bhatias are all Hindus' (Ibid: 65). It is, therefore, not surprising that 'joys and sorrows of one caste are not the joys and sorrows of another; one caste has no concern with other castes' (Ibid: 65).

Even in terms of social utility, Ambedkar argued, there is no positive story, because 'caste divides labourers, caste dissociates work from interest, caste disconnects intelligence from manual labour, caste devitalizes by denying to him the right to cultivate vital interest, and caste prevents mobilization' (Ibid: 67). For example, a rapidly changing modern industrial society expects that an individual must be free to change his occupations; but 'the caste system will not allow Hindus to take occupations where they are wanted if they do not belong to them by heredity' ; in fact, individual sentiment, individual preference has no place in the caste system; it is based on the 'dogma of predestination' (Ibid: 68). In other words, it is against the spirit of modernity.

It is now becoming clear that it was not easy for the wavelengths of Gandhi and Ambedkar to merge. Gandhi was a 'sanatani Hindu'; Ambedkar was uncompromising in his critique of Hinduism. Gandhi—with his deep spiritual longing—could reinterpret the *Bhagavad Gita*, find possibilities in the *Vedas* and the *Upanishads*, and radiate the message of love, harmony and togetherness; Ambedkar was a modernist, and relentlessly critical of the entire Hindu heritage—its *dharmashastras*, its epics, its fundamental texts. Gandhi believed in the possibility of changing people's conscience for removing the evil of untouchability; Ambedkar refused to be convinced, and saw it as a fad. No wonder then, Ambedkar critiqued and debunked Gandhi. It is impossible for the untouchables, Ambedkar used to say, to regard Gandhi as their friend. 'How can they believe him to be their friend when he wishes to retain caste and abolish untouchability, when it is clear that untouchability is only an extended form of caste and that therefore without abolition of caste there is no hope of abolition of untouchability' (Ambedkar, Vol. 9, 1991: 260)? For Ambedkar, there was no hope in Gandhi's anti-untouchability campaign. Because 'the Hindus to whom he appeals ...do not respond'; they hear his 'after-prayer sermons for a few minutes and then go to the comic opera, and there is nothing more to it' (Ibid: 263). Moreover, 'Gandhi does not wish to antagonize the Hindus even if such antagonism was necessary to carry out his anti-untouchability programme' (Ibid: 263). Ambedkar, it seems, was never tired of using excessively harsh words against Gandhi. 'Barring the illusory campaign against untouchability', wrote Ambedkar, 'Gandhism is another form of Sanatanism which is the ancient name for militant orthodox Hinduism' (Ibid: 295). Not solely that. 'All that Gandhism has done is to find a philosophic justification for Hinduism and its dogmas' (Ibid: 296). And hence 'the only reaction and a very natural reaction of the untouchables would be to run away from Gandhism' (Ibid: 297).

We know that we are living in a society in which the assertion of identity politics often leads to stereotypes, and generates an impression that there cannot be any bridge between Gandhi and Ambedkar, and we cannot live with both of them. I wish to contest this proposition. There are two reasons. First, Gandhi raised the moral question, and it was because of his illuminating presence in the nationalist movement that the plight of the untouchables became a major issue to reckon with. And Ambedkar came with a hammer, and aroused the confidence of the marginalized. Ambedkar without Gandhi would remain ghettoized; and Gandhi without Ambedkar would appear somewhat mild in his approach to the caste question. Second—and this is most important, even Ambedkar was destined to realize that religiosity, ethical sensibility and inner transformation were absolutely important for eradicating caste hierarchy. Gandhi with his dialogic religiosity (imagine his perpetual engagement with the *Bhagavad Gita* and *Sermon on the Mount*) and Ambedkar with his Buddhism were not really so different from each other, even though because of our narrow political interests we might feel tempted to erect a wall between the two. Look at Ambedkar's Buddhism. In a revealing essay on 'Buddha or Karl Marx', Ambedkar saw a great possibility in Buddha's method because 'his method was to change the mind of man, to alter his disposition so that whatever man does, he does it voluntarily without the use of force or compulsion' (Ambedkar, Vol. 3: 461). Was it altogether different from Gandhi's perpetual appeal to sharpen our moral conscience, and cultivate our 'soul-force'? I feel tempted to refer to a beautiful narrative that Ambedkar recalled in his *The Buddha and His Dhamma* (Vol. 11 1992: 185-86). Here is a story of Sunita who earned his living as a road sweeper in Rajagraha. One day in the early hours of the dawn the Buddha walked into Rajagraha for alms followed by a large number of Bhikkus. Sunita was cleaning the street, and collecting scraps and rubbish. He saw the Master; his mind was filled with joy; however, because of his low and hereditary occupation he was afraid. And 'finding no place to hide on the road, he placed his yoke in a bend in the wall and stood as if stuck to the wall, saluting the lord with clasped hands'. Then the Lord when he had come near, spoke to him in a voice divinely sweet, saying: 'Sunita, can you endure to leave home and come into the Order?' How could Sunita deny the Master's offering? It was a turning point in his life; the Master taught him the Dhamma and the Discipline. When asked how Sunita became so great, the Buddha said, 'As on a rubbish-heap on highway cast a lily may grow, fragrant and sweet, so among rubbish creatures, worldlings blind by insight shines the very Buddha's child'. Who would deny that a narrative of this kind which Ambedkar recalled so fondly reveals the power of love and compassion? Yes, love transcends barriers; without love legality is mere formality; politics is sterile; and struggle is mere bitterness. At one level Ambedkar spoke the language of rationality and modernity—liberty, equality and fraternity; but at another level he was speaking the language of religiosity—the language of Buddha. And it was not essentially different from that of Gandhi. Think of, for instance, Gandhi's days at Sevagram. Sevagram was an uncommonly backward village; the majority of its population consisted of Harijans who were not only denied access to temples, but could not avail themselves of the local priests, tailors, and barbers; they were forbidden to draw water from the wells, to send their children to schools, and even to use certain roads. But then, Gandhi sought to make a dent in this tyrannical system. He engaged Govind, a Harijan boy, to cook for him. He refused to have his hair cut by the village barber so long as he denied his services to Harijans. Despite high-caste opposition, he caused a private well in Sevagram to be opened to Harijans.

In a way, it was the spirit of love and compassion that enabled Gandhi to act, and make a difference. And that, I would argue, united Gandhi and Ambedkar. True, Ambedkar used terribly harsh words against Gandhi. 'The grace in Gandhism', he said, 'is a curse in its worst form; the virtue of the anti-Untouchability plank in Gandhism is quite illusory; there is no substance in it' (Vol. 9, 1991: 295). But then, why should we get carried away by such bitterness? After all, we should not forget that it was the same Ambedkar who, while celebrating Buddhism, wanted us to remember the Master's message: 'Beware of the anger of the tongue, and control thy tongue'!

## (IV)

Hierarchy, asymmetrical power relations, inequality and the quest for justice—in fact, the entire politico-ethical questions—take us to the notion of *order* and *conflict*, *system* and *anarchy*. Is it possible—or, for that matter, desirable—to celebrate the visions of solidarity and cohesiveness? Can love and good will unite us and generate waves of symmetry and fusion? Or, is it that the very idea of togetherness is illusory, there is no social equilibrium, there is only conflict and violence—manifest or latent, and this tension, far from being negative, is productive in the sense that it leads to radical social transformation? A question of this kind, we know, did bother sociologists and cultural anthropologists. It is in this context that I wish to refer to Emile Durkheim—his reflections on moral order and social solidarity.One thing that can be said categorically about this grand sociologist is that, for him, society is endowed with moral force; it transcends the individual; experiencing social solidarity is like experiencing the moral authority of the collective over the individual; this experience is sacred; and society reproduces itself through rites, rituals, ceremonies and festivals. In fact, his mega work on religion reveals this point rather sharply. Look at, for instance, totemism as an elementary form of religion. When someone worships a plant or an animal, is it an illusion? Religion, Durkheim sought to assert, is not an inexplicable hallucination; 'in fact, we can say that the believer is not deceived when he believes in the existence of a moral power upon which he depends and from which he receives all that is best in himself: this power exists, it is society' (Durkheim 1976: 225). The totem is merely a symbol; its sacred character is not implied in its intrinsic properties; it is sacred because it symbolizes the moral authority of society. And symbols are important because 'without symbols social sentiments could have only a precarious existence' (Ibid: 231). Social life in every period of history, said Durkheim, is made possible only by a vast symbolism. Totemism is just one example. We should not forget that 'collective sentiments can just as well become incarnate in persons or formulae: some formulae are flags, while there are persons, either real or mythical, who are symbols' (Ibid: 232).

In other words, be it a totem or a national flag, and all the rites, rituals and ceremonies centred on it, religiosity is an experience of the social bond, and it is sacred. God is social solidarity. No wonder, for Durkheim, 'the collective consciousness is the highest form of the psychic life, since it is the consciousness of the consciousness' (Ibid: 444).

At this juncture an important question arises: Is moral solidarity a misnomer in a modern society characterized by heightened individualism, personal autonomy and the doctrine of calculative, utilitarian economic exchange? Durkheim seemed to be acutely aware of this question. He distinguished 'organic solidarity' from 'mechanical solidarity'. Mechanical solidarity emerges out of resemblances and homogeneity of aspirations; no wonder, it is a distinctive feature of a simple, kinship-centric communitarian society. The story of a modern/industrial society is different. Here is a society characterized by massive differentiation, division of labour and specialized skills and aptitudes. Yet, as Durkheim wanted us to believe, solidarity is still possible because 'difference, as likeness, can be a cause of mutual attraction' (Durkheim 1969: 55). True, certain differences cause repulsion. Honest people, for instance, would find no affinity with hypocrites and pretenders. But then, there are differences that attract each other. Thus 'a theorist, a subtle and reasoning individual, often has a very special sympathy for practical men with their quick sense and rapid intuitions; the timid for the firm and the resolute, the weak for the strong, and conversely' (Ibid: 55). Indeed, 'we seek in our friends the qualities that we lack, since in joining with them, we participate in some measure in their nature and thus feel less incomplete' (Ibid: 56). This form of solidarity is called organic solidarity. See how it differs from mechanical solidarity. In the domain of mechanical solidarity 'the collective conscience completely envelops our whole conscience....our individuality is nil' (Ibid: 130). In contrast, organic solidarity is possible 'only if each one has a sphere of action which is peculiar to him; that is, a personality' (Ibid: 131). It is, therefore, necessary that 'the collective conscience leaves open a part of the individual conscience in order that special functions may be established there, functions which it cannot regulate' (Ibid: 131). Yet, this personal autonomy is not opposed to solidarity. Because each one depends more strictly on society as labour is more divided. And this solidarity too has its moral element; it cannot be equated with a contract, a business agreement. Not surprisingly, Durkheim evolved a sharp critique of Spencer's utilitarianism, and his notion of an atomized individual concerned primarily with his own interests. This sort of utilitarianism implies that social solidarity is nothing but the spontaneous accord of individual interests. However, as Durkheim cautioned us, solidarity based on selfish interests has no depth; it is superficial and transient because 'there is nothing less constant than interest; today it unites me to you; tomorrow it will make me your enemy' (Ibid: 204). Moreover, this sort of contract hides a latent conflict because 'where interest is the only ruling force each individual finds himself in a state of war with every other since nothing comes to mollify the egos, and any truce in this eternal antagonism would not be of long duration' (Ibid: 203-4). It is, therefore, important to remember that 'even where society relies most completely upon the division of labour, it does not become a juxtaposed atom, between which it can establish only external, transient contacts; rather the members are united by ties which extend deeper and far beyond the short moments during which the exchange is made' (Ibid: 227). In other words, unlike Spencer, Durkheim was striving for moral solidarity; every society, for him, is a moral society. After all, 'men cannot live together without acknowledging, and consequently, making mutual sacrifices, without tying themselves to one another with strong, durable bonds' (Ibid: 228). In a modern society the nature of solidarity has changed; but it has not lost its moral character. When individuals with different skills and aptitudes cooperate, it cannot be seen as a mere utilitarian/calculative move because 'cooperation also has its intrinsic morality' (Ibid: 228). This doesn't mean that individuals lose creativity and vitality; instead, the beauty of organic solidarity is that 'society learns to regard its members no longer as things over which it has rights, but as cooperators whom it cannot neglect and towards whom it owes duties' (Ibid: 228).

This leads to yet another important question: What happens if the degree of solidarity begins to reduce, and society loses its moral authority? As Durkheim would have argued, it leads to disastrous consequences; it stimulates inflated egos; it causes disintegration; and as a result, individuals miss what they need at the moment of crisis: the moral support of the community that restrains, regulates, appeases, connects and restores cohesiveness. Anyone familiar with Durkheim's revealing work on suicide would know how deeply he was concerned with this crisis, particularly relating to 'egoistic' and 'anomic' suicide in modern times. Modernity, we know, is not possible without personal autonomy and freedom; individualism is related to it. Individualism is not necessarily egoism. However, as Durkheim reminded us, it can be reduced to egoism in societies and environments 'where man is a God to mankind, the individual is readily inclined to consider the man in himself as a God and to regard himself as the object of his own cult' (Durkheim, 2006: 331).And when it happens individuals lose the rhythm of connectedness that can support them at the moment of crisis, and they find no reason 'to endure life's sufferings patiently'. As 'admitted masters of their destinies' they feel that 'it is their privilege to end their lives', and the result is the increasing rate of egoistic suicide. It should not be forgotten that the bond that unites individuals with a common cause 'attaches them to life, and the lofty goal they envisage prevents their feeling personal troubles so deeply'; in fact, a 'cohesive and animated society' generates a 'mutual moral support' which 'instead of throwing the individual on his own resources, leads him to share in the collective energy and supports his own when exhausted' (Ibid: 168). Durkheim noticed yet another disturbing trend in modern times—the 'dogma of economic materialism'. It intensifies greed; it increases desire; it knows no limit; 'nothing can calm it, since its goal is far beyond all it can attain' (Ibid: 216). See its consequences. A thirst arises for 'novelties, unfamiliar pleasures, nameless sensations', and all these new sensations 'cannot form a solid foundation of happiness to support one during days of trial'; weariness brings disillusionment; one cannot in the end 'escape the futility of an endless pursuit' (Ibid: 217). For Durkheim, 'since this disorder is greatest in the economic world, it has most victims there'; no wonder, 'industrial and commercial functions are really among the occupations which furnish the greatest number of suicides' (Ibid: 218).

In Emile Durkheim we see this deep concern. Society, for him, is moral; social solidarity is sacred; individualism should not be degenerated into egoism; and even a modern/secular society needs religiosity in terms of its engagement with the sacred, be it in the form of a flag, a shared history, a cherished memory that symbolizes the moral authority of the collective over the individual. He would not feel happy if the intensity of solidarity declines, society loses its moral sanctity, and disconnected individuals reduce it into a battle-field.

This urge to retain and sanctify social solidarity and order is often seen in sociological discourses. Durkheim created a solid foundation. And Talcott Parsons—a towering figure in 20th century American sociology—emerged as a grand theoretician creating the design of a perfectly ordered social system. Here is a sophisticated system. Making sense of it requires an understanding of what he regarded as 'action'. Action implies an agent—an actor. It must have an 'end'—a future state of affairs towards which the process of action is oriented. It must be initiated in a situation which consists of two parts— (a)those over which the actor has no control, or conditions; and (b) those over which he has control, or the means. Moreover, in the choice of alternative means to the end, there is a 'normative orientation'. While evolving his theory of action, Parsons showed his immense scholarship, and engaged in a critical dialogue with utilitarianism, positivism and idealism. (Parsons 1949). From all these approaches he learned what, he felt, ought to be learned, and rejected what couldn't be fitted into his order of things. He appreciated the importance the utilitarian system attaches to the zeal of actors—the way they strive for goals, and make choices over the means. However, he was worried that a purely utilitarian act would lead to unregulated/atomistic behaviour; it would cause a problem of order. He looked at the positivistic system; and, as he appreciated, it draws attention to the physical parameters of social life, and to the deterministic impact of these parameters on actions. But then, as he cautioned, its inherent reductionism and obsession with cause-effect relationships ignore the complex symbolic functionings of the human mind. No wonder, in order to overcome these limitations he referred to Durkheim—the importance he attached to the moral/symbolic element, and its normative values. Finally, from the Weberian idealistic tradition he learned the subjective reference to the theory of action. As Parsons would like us to believe, his theory of action is 'voluntaristic'.Here is an actor with a sense of freedom and subjectivity; he is not a robot or a puppet. However, he is not an atomized actor concerned primarily with his own pleasure; he knows the determining situations; and above all, he is aware of the presence of the plurality of actors, and he realizes that he is not insulated, and he is rooted in shared values and norms. In a way, Parsons was seeking to reconcile freedom and responsibility, agency and order, subjectivity and the facticity of the normative order. At this juncture, it becomes easier to understand the Parsonian grand social system. Imagine a situation. I am a teacher. I have arrived at the lecture hall to deliver a lecture. I find myself amidst my students. My action—delivering a lecture—cannot be separated from the presence of students, their expectations from me, and my expectations from them. And as a result, we begin to follow some shared norms; I switch off my mobile phone; and I expect them to do so; while I speak, I want them to remain silent; and they expect that while they ask questions, I answer with all sincerity. In other words, in the lecture hall many actors are interacting, and this interaction acquires a reasonably stable character because we reduce the possibility of random behaviour by following shared norms and practices. In a way, we see a social system emerging in the lecture hall. 'A social system', as Parsons defined, 'consists in a plurality of individual actors interacting with each other in a situation... defined and mediated in terms of a system of culturally structured and shared symbols' (Parsons 1951: 5-6). It is obvious that for a social system to function we need motivated actors and well-defined cultural symbols that can unite these actors into a coherent whole. No wonder, Parsons put great emphasis on 'the personality systems of the individual actors and the cultural system which is built into their action' (Ibid: 6). For example, an actor's personality system has to be developed so that he can be motivated to perform which is necessary for the system. This means that biological prerequisites of individual life, like nutrition and physical safety, and subtler needs like affection, support and security ought to be satisfied. Likewise, there are minimum social conditions necessary for the production, maintenance and development of the cultural system. To begin with, it is important to see that the communication system is not disrupted; no social system is possible 'without language, and without certain other minimum patterns of culture, such as empirical knowledge necessary to cope with situational exigencies, and sufficiently integrated patterns of expressive symbolism and value orientation' (Ibid: 34). Furthermore, we shouldn't forget that 'without the requisite cultural resources to be assimilated through internalization it is not possible for a human level of personality to emerge and hence for a human type of social system to develop' (Ibid: 34).

This implies that for a perfect social system to emerge

what is important is the integration of motivational and cultural elements. How can this integration take place? Yes, the attitude of expediency plays a role. Let us come back to the example of the lecture hall once again. Suppose I follow the university norm and deliver my lectures regularly because I think that teaching this particular course would help me to improve my bio-data, or enable me to get a promotion, or visit abroad. Here my orientation is essentially instrumental. But then, as Parsons would argue, we have to see beyond the instrumental logic; what is really important is 'introjection or internalization of the standard so that to act in conformity with it becomes a need-disposition in the actor's own personality structure, relatively independent of any instrumentally significant consequences of that conformity' (Ibid: 37). In other words, to refer to the earlier example, I need to follow the university norm quite naturally and spontaneously without bothering about its immediate instrumental gains. When this happens we can be sure of a meaningful integration of motivation with a normative pattern-structure of values. It is obvious that for retaining 'order' Parsons would plead for diverse 'mechanisms of socialization'; and socialization as a lifelong process takes place in multiple sites—families, schools, work places. Moreover, without the 'mechanisms of social control', as we are told by functionalist theories, no order is possible. Parsons was aware of the fact that 'no social system is perfectly equilibrated and integrated; deviant motivational factors are always operating' (Ibid: 298). Deviance, said Parsons, manifests itself in strain, and strain provokes 'anxiety, fantasy, hostile or aggressive hitting-back or hitting out reactions' (Ibid: 299). How do we control it? It is interesting to look at his recommendations. Instead of violent measures, he spoke of 'support'; it generates a sense of security, some sort of reassurance; it leads to the 'incorporation or retention of ego in a solidarity relationship'. We see its example in 'the stability of love attitudes of the mother in critical phases of socialization, or the collectivity-orientation of the therapist, his readiness to help and his understanding of the patient' (Ibid: 298). And this system of support can be more effective if there is also an element of 'permissiveness'. After all, we should not forget that people under strain do things which they would not have done under normal circumstances. That is why, 'permissiveness is to be interpreted as toleration of natural reactions to the frustration of expectations' (Ibid: 300). However, as Parsons reminded us, one should not forget to retain a balance between areas of permissiveness and of restriction on it. As an architect of the social system, Parsons spoke of many measures of social control. I wish to refer to what he regarded as the 'insulation' mechanisms. He spoke of crime and illness. A prison insulates and isolates the criminal; a hospital too insulates the patient. However, there is a qualitative difference between these two forms of insulation. Generally, the definition of the deviant as a criminal emphasizes the negative side. 'It constitutes a kind of extrusion from the social group with little concern for his return' (Ibid: 312). In other words, the criminal tends to be 'written off'. But the story of the 'sick role' is different. True, the hospital insulates the patient; yet, 'the sick role involves a relative legitimacy...so long as there is an implied agreement to pay the price in accepting certain disabilities and the obligation to get well' (Ibid: 312). There is hope; he can come back; herein lies the role of the physician, the therapist; they expose him to 'reintegrative' forces, and help him to break through the 'vicious circle of the generation of deviant motivation' (Ibid: 313). Here is a design of a reasonably integrated system. It was not that Parsons was altogether indifferent to social change; but his point of departure was the vision of equilibrium. Not surprisingly, a system of this kind would make us think that conflict is deviance, and it needs to be coped with in order to restore the coherence of the system.

Yes, order or social solidarity, it may be argued, is desirable. Imagine the state of French society in the late 19th/early 20th century; it was a society undergoing a process of rapid transformation. Durkheim, like Comte, needed moral order. Likewise, Parsons was required to keep the American dream alive in post-war/20th century America. Yet, the question is: can order exist in a world characterized by asymmetry, inequality and hierarchy of power? Pleading for order in a divided society, it may be argued, is like speaking the language of the powerful; it is like retaining the status quo, and trivializing dissent as deviance. It is an *ideology* that falsifies the reality, and hides its actual contradictions. It is, therefore, argued that conflict is real; conflict exists because of class divisions, because of all forms of social stratification and asymmetrical power relations. And conflict may be seen as a driving force for social transformation. What we regard as radical politics is based on this conflict theory—conflict between the colonizer and the colonized, conflict between landless peasants and feudal landlords, conflict between displaced *adivasis* and corporate elites pleading for 'development', conflict between subjugated women and privileged men in a patriarchal society, conflict between the dominant community and marginalized ethnic groups. And it is also possible to argue that violence is rooted in this conflict; and when the oppressed are forced to use violent strategies to overthrow the system, it should not be seen as pathological; instead, it may be felt as liberating and therapeutic.Enough has already been said and written about conflict, violence and liberation. Here I wish to refer to Fanon and Gandhi in order to reflect on this complex question that confronts our existence. Although their perceptions were situated in the politics of colonialism (Fanon was writing primarily about Algeria, its liberatarian struggle against the French colonial regime, and Gandhi, we know, grew with his experience in South Africa and colonial India)—its asymmetrical power relations and violence, the insights we gain would help us to throw light on any other conflict-ridden situation. To begin with, I feel tempted to quote from Jean- Paul Sartre's brilliantly written preface to Frantz Fanon's *The Wretched of the Earth*: 'No gentleness can efface the marks of violence; only violence itself can destroy them. The native cures himself of colonial neurosis by thrusting out the settler through force of arms. When his rage boils over, he rediscovers his lost innocence and he comes to know himself in that he himself creates his self...It achieves, slowly but surely, the emancipation of the rebel, for bit by bit it destroys in him and around him the colonial gloom' (Fanon 1983: 18). For Sartre, this violence is emancipatory; it cannot be devalued or condemned. As he added: 'If violence began this very evening and if exploitation and oppression had never existed on the earth, perhaps the slogan of non-violence might end the quarrel. But if the whole regime, even your non-violent ideas are conditioned by a thousand-year-old oppression, your passivity serves only to place you in the ranks of the oppressors' (Ibid: 21). We know that Fanon's training in psychiatry made him realize that colonialism denies the colonized all attributes of humanity; it forces the people it dominates to ask themselves the question constantly: 'In reality, who am I' (Ibid: 200)? See its consequences. I wish to refer to an illustration Fanon gave: 'The murder by two young Algerians thirteen and fourteen years old respectively of their European playmate' (Ibid: 217-19). One of them was asked; 'Does having killed somebody worry you'? 'No', he replied, 'since they want to kill us, so...'Not solely that. He was asked: 'Do you mind being in prison'? And his reply was categorically clear: 'No'. Reflect on the anguish of the second boy: 'Two of my family members were killed. At home, they said that the French had sworn to kill us all, one after the other. And did they arrest a single Frenchman for all those Algerians who were killed'? He was reminded of his childhood, and told that this sort of thing should concern only grown-up people, not a child like him. But he was not convinced. 'They kill children too. So I killed him. Now you can do what you like'. Here is a situation that defies the Durkheimian 'moral order', or the Parsonian grand 'social system'. Is it just a state of mental disorder, or something far deeper? What needs to be understood is that here violence is real, intimate, experiential. The suppressed fury of the colonized is trying to find an outlet. As Fanon said, 'Colonialism is not a thinking machine, nor a body endowed with reasoning faculties. It is violence in its natural state, and it will only yield when confronted with greater violence' (Ibid: 48). No wonder, as Fanon thought, 'the colonized man finds his freedom in and through violence' (Ibid: 68). Violence, for him, is a 'cleansing' force. 'It frees the native from his inferiority complex and from his despair and inaction; it makes him fearless and restores his self-respect' (Ibid: 74).

Fanon made us sensitive; he enabled us to see beyond the 'law and order'discourse which the status quo often uses to subdue the powerless; he wanted to tell us that not all forms of violence are necessarily immoral; when the oppressed use violence to liberate themselves, its therapeutic possibilities ought to be felt and understood. Gandhi, however, took us to a different domain. Like Fanon, he too experienced colonialism, its violence, its asymmetrical power relations; yet, the art of resistance he pleaded for and practised was inseparable from *ahimsa* and *satyagraha*. I recall an insightful article *The Doctrine of the Sword* Gandhi wrote in 1920. To begin with, it is important to understand the deeper meaning of non-violence. It is not an escape from conflict; it is not an illusion that everything is peaceful; it is not a legitimation for cowardice. 'When my eldest son', as Gandhi reminded us, 'asked me what he should have done, had he been present when I was fatally assaulted in 1908, whether he should have run away and seen me killed or whether he should have used his physical force which he could and wanted to use, and defended me, I told him that it was his duty to defend me even by using violence' (Gandhi in Murti 1970: 145). Gandhi would prefer violence where there is only a choice between cowardice and violence. It is, therefore, important to realize that non-violence does not mean 'meek submission to the will of the evil-doer, but it means the pitting of one's whole soul against the will of the tyrant' (Ibid: 146). And hence it is 'infinitely superior to violence' (Ibid: 145). To realize the strength of non-violence is to recognize that one is not a lump of flesh; one is essentially a soul 'that cannot perish and that can rise triumphant above every physical weakness and defy the physical combination of a whole world' (Ibid: 146). True, the path of non-violence is immensely difficult; violence may give immediate results. 'If India takes up the doctrine of the sword', Gandhi acknowledged, 'she may gain momentary victory' (Ibid: 147). However, his goal was different. Call it whatever you like—courage or naïve dream or prophetic insight; he could say: 'I take pride in looking upon India as my country because I believe that she has it in her to demonstrate to the world the supremacy of soul-force' (Ibid: 150). Soul-force, unlike brute force, means the ability to win over others by the 'power of love'; it is 'the virtue of the brave'. We know that Fanon appealed to the colonized not to imitate Europe—the site of brute colonial masters. 'European techniques and the European style ought no longer to tempt us and to throw us off our balance' (Fanon 1983: 252). But then, how could the colonized use the same strategy of violence which was the essence of colonial European power? Here Fanon failed; and Gandhi's answer was more convincing and daring: 'I believe absolutely that India has a mission for the world. She is not to copy Europe blindly. India's acceptance of the doctrine of the sword will be the hour of my trial' (Gandhi in Murti 1970: 147). In a conflict-ridden society, we keep debating on diverse strategies for a liberatarian movement. In a country like ours characterized by gross inequality and exploitation, we experience violence, be it the violence perpetuated by the state, or the counter-violence by the Maoists or other radical groups. Under these circumstances, it is for each sensible person to decide how he or she reads Fanon and Gandhi. One thing is, however, clear. In the name of Durkheimian or Parsonian order, we cannot overlook the reality of conflict.

At the same time, it is equally important to realize that the new society that radical politics dreams of and strives for is not conflict-ridden; instead, it is some sort of a secular paradise. Ambedkarites want a casteless society; feminists want a society that takes us beyond the oppressive duality of patriarchy, and celebrates a harmonic/symmetrical man-woman relationship; and the Marxian utopia speaks of a communist society transcending all dualities. In other words, it is a journey from conflict to integration, from asymmetry to symmetry, from violence to peace. To put it otherwise, at a deeper level the choice is not between the functionalist theory and conflict theory, between order and chaos; the real choice is between superficial order and meaningful order, between order as domination and order as creative fulfilment. It is in this context that we can say that a just society is one that has its own rhythm of order: the kind of order that emanates from man's freedom, his creative fulfilment, his art of relatedness, his ability to love and give, not possess and dominate. Is it only about politics? Or, is it also about spiritual longing? Should the proponents of radical politics give a break, and reflect on this spiritual quest? At this juncture, we need to reflect on order and anarchy, freedom and discipline, love and communism.

Here Sri Aurobindo—an extraordinarily illuminating mystic/philosopher—becomes immensely relevant. Aurobindo visualized the ideal of human unity, reflected on diversity and oneness, freedom and order. 'Unity we must create, but not necessarily uniformity', said Aurobindo. This implies that we must be careful about an imposed order which 'discourages the principle of natural growth which is the true method of life' (Sri Aurobindo 1977: 404). In fact, as we are reminded, nature teaches us a great lesson; it reveals how true unity emanates from a rich diversity. 'Nature does not manufacture, does not impose a pattern or a rule from outside; she impels life to grow from within' (Ibid: 403). In the name of restoring 'order' we shouldn't negate the principle of nature. Aurobindo wanted us to cherish the idea that 'the ultimate aim of nature must be to develop the individual and all individuals to their full capacity, to develop the community and all communities to the full expression of that many-sided existence and potentiality which their differences were created to express, and to evolve the united life of mankind to its full common capacity and satisfaction, not by the suppression of the fullness of life of the individual or the smaller community, but by full advantage taken of the diversity which they develop' (Ibid: 400). No wonder, his vision was against the kind of order that the state seeks to impose on people. The state is not an organism; it is a machinery; and 'it tries to manufacture, but what humanity is here to do is to grow and create' (Ibid: 283). When the organized state becomes overwhelmingly powerful it eliminates free individual effort. The state has no soul; it is a collective egoism; and 'it amounts to giving up the present form of individual egoism into another, a collective form larger but not superior, rather in many ways inferior to the best individual egoism' (Ibid:

282). That is why, even though it justifies its existence by organizing the economic well-being of the community, it is bound to act crudely because 'it is incapable of that free, harmonious and intelligently or instinctively varied action which is proper to organic growth' (Ibid: 283). It is difficult to imagine a healthy unity by the state machinery; we ought to strive for a 'moralized and even spiritualized humanity united in its true soul and not only in its outward life and body' (Ibid: 284).

There is no conflict between order and freedom; in fact, 'the truest order is that which is founded on the greatest possible liberty' (Ibid: 490). How is it possible? For Aurobindo, the answer lies not in reason, but in the soul of man. When man realizes the fundamental oneness of existence, he finds no contradiction between his inner growth and the creative fulfilment of the collectivity. And this collective awakening, as Aurobindo elaborated in *The Human Cycle*, requires an evolution from the infrarational stage to the rational stage to the suprarational/supramental existence. In the infrarational stage men are not capable of referring their life and action in its principles and its forms to the judgment of clarified intelligence; they act principally out of their instincts and impulses. However, in a rational stage man's intelligent will 'becomes the judge, arbiter and presiding motive of his thought, feeling and action, the moulder, destroyer and re-creator of his leading ideas, aims and intuitions' (Aurobindo 1977: 173). In a way what we regard as modernity reaffirms the Age of Reason. Here is a world that celebrates the power of science, its rational/analytical discourse, its objectivity, its empiricism. It is indeed a step forward. It has produced great scientists, technologists, economists; it has evolved from the physical to the vital to the mental stage. But, as Aurobindo would argue, this cannot be the final stage of evolution. We are destined to move further, experience the psychic stage of being, and arrive at the Spiritual Age. He showed the crisis of modernity, the discontents implicit in the Age of Reason. Take, for instance, the principle of individualistic democracy—a major socio-political articulation of modernity. It believes in liberty and freedom; it assumes that everyone is important in shaping our collective affairs. However, freedom cannot operate only in the domain of the intellect; it cannot be the freedom of a discrete ego. True freedom is spiritual freedom that nurtures collective ecstasy. Not surprisingly, in the absence of spiritual freedom individualistic democracy fails to connect one's freedom with the freedom of all; it misses the spirit of love and care; it leads to some sort of social Darwinism, a culture of reckless competition. And it ends in 'the survival not of the spiritually, rationally or physically fittest, but of the most fortunate and vitally successful' (Ibid: 186). This crisis leads to yet another quest: the search for democratic socialism. Herein lies yet another politico-economic articulation of the Age of Reason. It seeks to overcome the limitations of democratic individualism—its inequality and conflict. It pleads for an organized state for bringing about equality. But then, as Aurobindo reminded us, in the absence of the awakening of the spirit, even democratic socialism degenerates into totalitarianism. To borrow his prophetic words, 'there is a rapid crystallization of the social, economic, political life of the people into a new rigid organization effectively controlled at every point; there is the compulsory casting of thought, education, expression, action into a set of iron mould, a fixed system of ideas and life-motives, with a fierce and ruthless, often a sanguinary repression of all that denies and differs; there is a total unprecedented compression of the whole communal existence so as to compel a maximum efficiency and a complete unanimity of mind, speech, feeling, life' (Ibid: 193). The question is if democratic collectivism too fails to make good, where do we go? Does it mean that the Age of Reason cannot unite the principles of liberty, equality and fraternity? Possibly this means that a perfect reconciliation between order and freedom, differences and equality cannot emanate from the discourse of reason; we ought to evolve further; we should become ready 'to take up the spiral of human evolution where the curve of the Age of Reason naturally ends by its own normal evolution and make ready the ways of a deeper spirit' (Ibid: 194). We shouldn't forget that 'reason is neither the first principle of life, nor can be its last, supreme and sufficient principle' (Ibid: 202). As a matter of fact, 'the solution lies not in the reason but in the soul of man, in its spiritual tendencies' (Ibid: 206). Neither a totalitarian state nor a cult of egoistic individualism, but it is a spiritual or an inner freedom that creates a perfect human order. This is a journey towards the Spiritual Age. This means an awakening of 'the love which is founded of a deeper truth of our being,...the spiritual comradeship which is the expression of an inner realization of oneness' (Ibid: 207). Only then is it possible that 'the true individualism of the unique godhead in each man finds itself on the true communism of the equal godhead in the race' (Ibid: 207). Does it then mean that the material domain of conflict—the hard reality of socio-economic and political discrimination—has to be overlooked? Certainly not. It means that no revolution is possible without inner awakening, flowering. Love unites the material and the spiritual, diversity and oneness. Love is revolution; revolution is love.

In fact, Sri Aurobindo's spiritual anarchism gave us a new ideal to strive for—an ideal that could not be visualized through the paradigm of modernist sociology, be it the functionalist preoccupation with order or the criticality of the conflict theory. Are we then entering the domain of love, the ecstasy of togetherness, the ultimate experience of overcoming all boundaries?

## (V)

There are many constraints. Imagine what we regard as *desire*—an important component of our earthly existence. It is this desire—aggressive desire for wealth, fame, success—that acts as a stumbling block, erects a wall, and disrupts the flow of love. But then, as it is said, it is impossible to imagine human existence without desire. Because the very materiality/physicality of life leads to desire; in order to sustain and reproduce ourselves we need things; we need food, clothing, shelter, medicine; and as life evolves a series of new needs emerge: education, aesthetics, culture, improved lifestyle. To live is to need things; but then, the magnitude of what we need crosses all limits. As we look at our own times, we see this ongoing play of desire, how it multiplies, and takes us to a world from where there seems to be no return. We desire ever-changing technologies; we desire fashionable goods and commodities; we desire images, symbols, spectacles. All our supermarkets and malls, the blooming real estate business, the proliferation of the beauty industry—everything seems to indicate that it is desire—the desire to have more and more—that leads to this massive techno-economic development. It is said that man—modern man pursuing the project of 'development' and 'progress'—must be active, ambitious, competitive, future-oriented. There is no limit to desire; no limit to growth; no limit to our capacity to consume!

Herein lies the need for caution. It is not always possible to realize when natural needs end, and we fall into the trap of *greed*. When it happens we get caught into a vicious circle. One desire leads to another; it is the restless mind that needs more and more. It is indeed difficult to understand when all this happens—when the simple need for transportation loses its simplicity, and becomes a desire for every new model of car we see in the street; when the natural urge to have a simple home loses its beauty, and the mythology of a 'dream home' that the real estate business propagates enters our consciousness; when commodities transcend their use value, and begin to seduce us because of the symbols they emit—the symbols of masculinity, sexuality, cultural distinction, lifestyle. As Herbert Marcuse said with great insight, while 'true' needs are the vital ones—nourishment, clothing, lodging at an attainable level of culture, 'false' needs are superimposed upon the individual, these are the needs that perpetuate 'toil, aggressiveness, misery and injustice'; in fact,'most of the prevailing needs to relax, to have fun, to behave and consume in accordance with the advertisements, to love and hate what others love and hate belong to the category of false needs' (Marcuse 2002: 7). When this happens the lightness of being disappears; life becomes a ceaseless exercise in earning, saving, insuring, shopping and consuming. There is no sunrise, no sunset, no full moon in malls; there is no poetry in the real estate enterprise; there is no music in the stock exchange. There is only noise, anxiety, restlessness—the curve of success and failure, euphoria and depression. Development becomes inseparable from suffering, and 'domination—in the guise of affluence and liberty—extends to all spheres of private and public existence' (Ibid: 20).

However, there are reminders. The Buddhists have said it so profoundly that it is desire that is the root of suffering; we desire; we get attached; we confuse what is temporal and transient with something that is eternal; and hence this perpetual pain and *dukkha* resulting from the loss of what is essentially impermanent—our wealth, our possessions, our ego, our success. This also leads to terrible fear, anxiety and insecurity. No *nivarna* is possible without awareness, without freedom from this cycle of desire and samsara. There is no greater happiness, as we are reminded, than the happiness of freedom from selfish attachments to all that is impermanent and ever-changing; there is no wealth greater than the wealth of contentment; there is no bliss higher and more abiding than the bliss of *nirvana*. It is in this context that I feel inspired to refer to the *Brhadaranyak Upanishad*—particularly the conversation between Yajnavalkya and his wife Maitreyi (BU: II.4.1- II.4.5). 'Maitreyi', said Yajnavalkya, 'I am about to go forth from this state of householder. Look, let me make a final settlement between you and Katyayani'. But then, Maitreyi asked: 'If, indeed, Venerable Sir, this whole earth filled with wealth were mine, would I be immortal through that?' 'No', replied Yajnavalkya, 'like the life of the rich even so would your life be. Of immortality, however, there is no hope through wealth'. Then Maitreyi said: 'What should I do with that by which I do not become immortal? Tell me that, indeed, Venerable Sir, of what you know of the way to immortality'. And finally, Yajnavalkya replied: 'Verily, not for the sake of the husband is the husband dear but a husband is dear for the sake of the Self. Verily, not for the sake of the wife is the wife dear but a wife is dear for the sake of the Self....Verily, not for the sake of wealth is wealth dear but wealth is dear for the sake of the Self....Verily, not for the sake of the worlds are the worlds dear but the worlds are dear for the sake of the Self. Verily, not for the sake of the gods are the gods dear but the gods are dear for the sake of the Self. Verily, not for the sake of all is all dear but all is dear for the sake of the Self. Verily, O Maitreyi, it is the Self that should be seen, heard of, reflected on and meditated upon. Verily, by the seeing of, by the hearing of, by the thinking of, by the understanding of the Self, all this is known'. The message is clear. There is a deeper purpose of human existence; it is to overcome limitedness, and experience eternal bliss in becoming one with the Infinite. There seems to be no end to such reminders. 'Greed for more and more', as the Quran reveals, 'distracted you from God till you reached the grave. But you will soon come to know. Indeed, were you to know the truth with certainty, you would see the fire of Hell. You would see it with the eye of certainty. Then on that Day you shall be questioned about your worldly favours' (Khanam 2012 : 471). Or, for that matter, see John's beautiful message in the Bible: 'Do not love the world or anything in the world. If anyone loves the world, the love of the Father is not in him. For everything in the world—the cravings of sinful man, the lust of his eyes and the boasting of what he has and does—comes not from the Father but from the world. The world and its desires pass away, but the man who does the will of God lives forever' (Bible: John 2.15).

Yet, we forget; we remain indifferent; the game continues. Is it because of what is often being legitimated as 'development' and its obvious byproduct: the culture of consumption? At this juncture, it is important to recall Erich Fromm's brilliant analysis of 'having' mode of existence. Indeed, 'in a culture in which the *supreme goal is to have—and to have more and more—and in which one can speak of someone as being worth a million dollars'*, said Fromm, 'it would seem that the very essence of being is having; that if one *has* nothing, one *is* nothing' (Fromm 1982: 25). No wonder, the attitude inherent in such a culture is that of 'swallowing the whole world; the consumer is the eternal suckling crying for the bottle' (Ibid: 36). Is it the reason that these days corruption does not shock us any more? We take it for granted that a politician has to use all his sources and contacts in order to earn as much as he can; a young IAS officer need not hesitate to take a lot of dowry, and reduce one of the most beautiful events in life into a business contract; and the aspiring middle class should find no problem in paying a huge capitation fee for getting an entry into private management/engineering colleges. Or, is it the reason that man can cheat a helpless victim even when the worst form of natural calamity makes things upside down? It is not my contention to argue that greed is something new; there was no mythical past or a 'golden' age free from all vices. However, the fact is that these days we find ourselves in a culture that normalizes the attitude to possess, to accumulate, to grab, to have; in fact, it sanctifies aggression, this reckless ambition. Have more and more. Restraint, limit, contentment—these are all bad, conservative. Demand more, possess more, conquer more. Have more wealth, more prosperity. Have more technologies: more cars, more computers, more mobiles, more cameras, more pictures. More fast food joints, more restaurants, more speed, more flyovers, more expressways, more electricity, more petrol, more nuclear energy. The story of 'more' keeps moving. No end, no rest, no looking back. Only eternal restlessness! And ironically, this culture of conquering leads to fear—fear of losing all that one has. Fromm asked: 'If I am what I have and if what I have is lost, who then am I'? And see the wisdom in his answer: 'Because I can lose what I have, I am necessarily constantly worried...I am afraid of thieves, of economic changes, of revolutions, of sickness, of death, and I am afraid of love, of freedom, of growth, of change, of the unknown... I become defensive, hard, suspicious, lonely, driven by the need to have more in order to be better protected' (Ibid: 111). This is violence. First, we cause violence to ourselves. We negate our possibilities—our ability to experience peace, calmness and harmony. Fear, anxiety and a sense of perpetual insecurity envelop us from all sides. Second, we cause violence to others because everyone is a competitor either to be defeated, or to be used for purely instrumental purposes. As Fromm said, 'if everyone wants to have more, everyone must fear one's neighbour's aggressive intention to take away what one has'; no wonder, 'having relationships are heavy, burdened, filled with conflicts and jealousies' (Ibid: 114). And finally, we cause violence to mother earth; we destroy natural resources; we keep manipulating, controlling nature for fulfilling our ever-increasing greed. However, Fromm reconciled his humanism with his deep spiritual faith in human possibilities. He could inspire us to strive for the *being* mode of existence. This means the ability to live with the inner treasure rather than external possessions, the ability to love, find meaning and fulfilment in simple things, in relationships, in comradeship, in nature, in music, in aesthetics. Here, as Fromm said, 'my centre is within myself; my capacity for being and for expressing my essential powers is part of my character structure and depends on me' (Ibid: 112). As a result, one becomes free from fear and anxiety. 'If *I am who I am* and not what I have, nobody can deprive me or threaten my security and my sense of identity' (Ibid: 112). There is no sense of possession, no fear of losing; instead, the more you give the more you fulfil yourself. For one gifted with the being mode of existence, love overflows, spreads out. As Fromm said beautifully, 'the powers of reason, of love, of artistic and intellectual creation, all essential powers grow through the process of being expressed; what is spent is not lost, but on the contrary, what is kept is lost' (Ibid: 112). In other words, living life meaningfully is to celebrate the being mode of existence. However, most people find giving up their having orientation too difficult because 'what holds them back is the illusion that they could not walk by themselves, that they would collapse if they were not supported by the things they have' (Ibid: 93). But Fromm was convinced that 'the realization of the new society is possible only if the old motivations of profit and power are replaced by new ones: being, sharing, understanding; if the marketing character is replaced by the productive, loving character...' (Ibid: 196).

At this juncture, it is equally important to understand that Marx too was a spiritualist of some kind. Look at his moral critique of private property and possessiveness. Indeed, it has made us 'so stupid and one-sided that an object is only *ours* when we have it—when it exists for us as capital, or when it is directly possessed, eaten, drunk, worn, inhabited, etc., in short, when it is used by us' (Marx 1977: 101). It is like saying that I cannot smell the fragrance of a flower unless I pluck it, possess it, and keep it in my drawing room. In other words, I have lost my imagination; I have become poorer; I have become dull, insensitive, inert. 'In the place of all physical and mental senses there has therefore come the sheer estrangement of all these senses, the sense of *having*' (Ibid: 101). Not solely that. This sense of having, or this brute power of money destroys my *human* essence, and transforms everything into its contrary. 'I am *brainless*, but money is the *real brain* of all things and how then should its possessor be brainless'? (Ibid: 130). As Marx wrote with heightened sensitivity, money transforms 'fidelity into infidelity, love into hate, hate into love, virtue into vice, vice into virtue, servant into master, master into servant, idiocy into intelligence, and intelligence into idiocy' (Ibid: 132). To put it otherwise, I become what I am not; my esistence is pretentious, filled with heavy armour; I become a victim of my possession, my pride in the act of having, consuming, conquering. What then is the way out? For Marx from whom Fromm learned some of his lessons, the answer is nothing but love because 'you can exchange love only for love, trust for trust, etc' (Ibid: 132). My private property, my possessions, my money, my 'having' mode of existence wouldn't be able to give me what my authentic being needs: love, reciprocity, trust, beauty, aesthetics. It is only a living relationship with the world that can fulfil me. 'If you love without evoking love in return—that is, if your loving as loving does not produce reciprocal love; if through a *living expression* of yourself as a loving person you do not make yourself a *beloved one*', said Marx, 'then your love is impotent—a misfortune' (Ibid: 132).

Love is not possession. Love is not irresistible greed. Love is one's *being*, one's inner treasure—the ability to fulfil oneself in the act of melting, merging, giving. Love and a sense of narcissistic ego burdened with external possessions are contradictory. It was, therefore, not surprising that Gandhi ( who inspired a significant section of activists and theorists who critique the existing practice of development and its violence) was always critical of the dominant notion of economic progress; never did he lose an opportunity to remind us of the need to make a difference between 'moral progress' and mere 'material advancement without limit'. 'If I were not afraid of treading on dangerous ground, I would...show you that possession of riches has been a hindrance to real growth', Gandhi wrote in one of his articles on economic progress (Gandhi in Murti 1970: 294). We were told that we could not serve God and Mammon together. How nice it is to be reminded that we should show 'more truth than gold, greater fearlessness than pomp of power and wealth, greater charity than love of self' (Ibid: 297). In fact, Gandhi could not be imagined without his notion of *aparigraha* or non-possessiveness. It is a sense of possessiveness (or a sense of having) and resultant attachment to objects, things, wealth that cause bondage, intensify one's ego, generate fear, and lead to violence. Gandhi referred to the *Bhagavad Gita*, invoked the principle of *aparigraha*, and felt the futility of war because 'himsa is impossible without anger, without attachment, without hatred'.

This austerity should not mean the glorification of life-negating poverty. Instead, it should mean the ability to lead a life free from the burden of externalities—things, commodities, wealth.... This is lightness; and this lightness has its profound simplicity and beauty; and this is freedom because with lightness one has reduced one's dependence on the excesses of life; one has become a free bird flying, and experiencing the vastness of the blue sky. In the age of conspicuous consumption it is indeed refreshing to find someone who lives without artificial needs, who lives simply, beautifully, courageously. It is great to adore Gandhi's courage to believe that to remain 'voluntarily poor' is a higher ideal one should strive for.

Is it possible for a capitalist, as Gandhi wanted, to divest himself of exclusive ownership and declare himself to be in possession as a trustee for the people? For many, it is a naïve idea because, as it is argued, a capitalist is a capitalist precisely because he accumulates wealth, and exploits others; it is a structural problem; an attempt to alter the conscience of a capitalist is stupid. In the Marxian project of socialism it is the state that would abolish private property, and establish its hold over collective property for distributive justice. But then, Gandhi was not naïve. He acknowledged: 'It is highly probable that my advice will not be accepted and my dream will not be realized' (Ibid: 315). However, he raised a disturbing question: 'Who can guarantee that the socialist's dream will be realized' (Ibid: 316)? This question needs to be taken seriously. Is it possible for the socialist state to do justice to collective property? Or, is it that the socialist state creates its own power elite, its own notion of greed, violence and exploitation? Moreover, if this aggressive desire—desire for more wealth, more militaristic power—is shifted from the individual to the state, nothing fundamentally alters. The narcissistic state becomes equally greedy and violent. The idea of trusteeship may be naïve. However, what needs to be realized is that no revolution is possible without a moral/ethical/spiritual transformation of each of us; and this is possible when we experience the meaning of yet another mode of existence: simple, rhythmic, musical living without the narcissistic ego, without possessions, without the golden cage of consumption. 'Socialism', wrote Gandhi, 'is explicit in the first verse of the Ishopanishad' (Ibid: 316). In other words, it is not a game to be seized; instead, we ought to realize the power of love which alone can take us beyond our limited selves, and enable us to expand our horizons.

## (VI)

Expansion, it is said, is not easy. We erect walls, separate ourselves from others, and legitimate this limitedness in the name of *identity*. See its paradox. My social identity enables me to define myself with reference to others. It gives me a sense of belonging, a shared heritage, a culture; it reduces the possibility of randomness in my social practices; it stabilizes and consolidates my existence. Hence when I say that I am a Hindu or a Muslim, a Brahmin or a Dalit, an Indian or an American, I feel myself assured. I feel that I have my 'community'—its shared history and memory; and its distinctive mark—be it language, caste, religion, nationality, iconic figure—'protects' me from uncertainty, from the difficult task of defining my life-project every moment; I am like all those who carry the same identity mark; I say 'yes', and live the way they want; and hence I am 'normal', 'stable'! Yet, paradoxically, this very 'assurance' tends to separate me from others who appear to be different in terms of language, religion, ethnicity, caste, nationality; I fail to see beyond the visible differences; the deeper oneness remains beyond my cognition. In fact, my identity with all its distinctiveness asserts itself in finding its other, its opposite. And the act of blaming and stigmatizing the other gets intensified if the resources are unevenly distributed. The result is a mode of living centred heavily on one's social identity leading to what political sociologists regard as 'identity politics'; it is by no means liberating; it breeds the principle of exclusion, conflict and hatred. Its divisive character does not change even when it seeks to project itself as 'politically correct'.

But then, is it possible to live without an identity—a socially constituted, historically determined self? Possibly, it is not. We are social beings; we live in groups; and what we are—the language we speak, the religion we adhere to, the heroes we worship, the food we eat—cannot be understood without situating ourselves in the network of social relationships. As sociologists and social psychologists argue, 'self' is constituted in the process of interaction, in the act of internalizing societal values, aspirations, role-models, or what George Herbert Mead would have regarded as the 'generalized other'. Not surprisingly, we have our language, our religion, our nationality. We are not empty; we are already conditioned by our social selves and identities. Yet, there is an aspiration. We wish to overcome our conditionings, and embrace the larger world; we wish to unite the finite with the infinite, differences with deeper unity. Love is this aspiration, this awakening that I am not just my caste, my language, my nationality; I am something more; I am universal—unbounded energy. However, before we reflect on this possibility, it is important to remind ourselves of the pathology of a mode of a living which, in the name of fixed identity, blocks the flow of inner music, brutalizes one, and causes violence.

One carries multiple identities. Let me begin with myself. I have many identity cards. My university identity card reveals that I have a professional identity; I am a university professor. And I have a passport that indicates that India as a nation-state gives me my identity, and it alone can decide whether I can cross borders. Moreover, one can say that here is a person who is essentially a male/ Hindu/ Brahmin. I ask myself: Who am I? Am I predominantly a university professor, or an Indian national, or a Hindu, or a Brahmin? Or am I rather complex—living with many identities simultaneously without any defining centre? Or am I free, universal not carrying the heavy luggage of any particular identity? Or possibly I too wish to sing with Rumi: 'What can I do my friends, if I do not know? I am neither Christian nor Jew, nor Muslim nor Hindu. What can I do? What can I do?... My place is the placeless. My trace is the traceless' (Rumi in Jamal 2009: 140). This is not just my question; this is a question everyone ought to ask for herself because we are aware of the pathology of the rigidity of fixed identity and its inherent dualism; and at some finer moments even ordinary mortals like us realize the fusion of horizons. To begin with, think of a situation when, for specific socio-political circumstances, one particular identity becomes dominant, and begins to define and fix a person. Suppose I begin to see myself primarily in terms of my ascribed caste; caste decides my politics; caste dictates my social relationships; caste defines my worldview. And its consequences, as I have already narrated through the story of Premchand, are disastrous. I become, narrow, limited. I promote caste war, caste prejudice, caste politics, caste stereotypes. The irony is that even if in the name of liberating society from caste I use the category of caste, I fall into its trap. Or for that matter, imagine that my religion becomes my essential identity; my religion becomes my uniform, shapes my politics, constructs the discourse of my nationality, generates stereotypes of 'friends' and 'enemies'. Religion loses the quest, forgets the language: 'One I seek, One I know, One I see, One I call; He is the first, He is the last, He is the external, He is the innermost' (Ibid: 140); instead, religion becomes a bundle of external symbols and rituals through which differences are exaggerated, and hatred created. We have witnessed how disastrous it could be. I wish to refer to one of Sadat Hasan Manto's stories in order to understand this terrible degradation of humanity.

It was the time of religious nationalism—the doctrine of the 'two nation theory', the belief that Hindus and Muslims constitute two antagonistic nations; and it is impossible for them to live together. It was the time of partition—the experience of migration, displacement and homelessness, and resultant mistrust and violence. It was the time when, as Manto wrote in his characteristic style, a father would appeal: 'Don't kill my daughter in front of my eyes', and they would respond: 'All right, all right. Peel off her clothes and shoo her aside' (Manto in Hasan 2008: 406). It was the time when, to quote Manto again, 'the rioters brought the train to a stop; those who belonged to the other religion were methodically picked up and slaughtered; and after it was all over, those who remained were treated to a feast of milk, custard pies and fresh fruit' (Ibid: 407). It was the time when Manto narrated the story of *The Return* (Ibid: 39-41)—the return of a daughter from India to Pakistan. Yes, the special train left Amritsar at two in the afternoon, arriving at Lahore eight hours later. Many had been killed on the way. When Sirajuddin regained consciousness, he found himself lying on bare ground, surrounded by screaming men, women and children. Slowly a succession of images raced through his mind. Attack...fire...escape...railway station...night...Sakina. He rose abruptly, and started looking for Sakina; but she was nowhere to be found. Eventually everything came to him in a flash—the dead body of his wife, her stomach ripped open. Before her death she didn't forget to remind him: 'Leave me where I am. Take the girl away.' But then, where did Sakina disappear? Had he brought her as far as the railway station? Had she got into the carriage with him? When the rioters had stopped the train, had they taken her with them? There were no answers. Even his tears had dried up. However, one day he found a group of young men who claimed that they had brought back women and children left behind on the other side. With great hope Sirajuddin gave them a description of his daughter: 'Big eyes, black hair, a mole on the left cheek'. He blessed them with his prayer that they would succeed in finding her. And yes, one day they indeed found a girl on the roadside—a pretty girl with a mole on her left cheek... Meanwhile, many days had gone by and Sirajuddin had still not found any news of his daughter. And then, one day he saw them in a camp. They were about to drive away. He shouted; 'Have you found Sakina, my daughter?' 'We will, we will', they replied all together. Sirajuddin continued to hope and pray. And finally, it happened. It was evening. He saw four men carrying the body of a young girl found unconscious near the railway tracks; they were taking her to the camp hospital. Yes, it was a young woman with a mole on her left cheek. It was Sakina. Meanwhile, she moved slightly; her hands groped for the cord which kept her shalwar tied round her waist; with painful slowness she unfastened it, pulled the garment down and opened her thighs. 'She is alive. My daughter is alive,'Sirajuddin shouted with joy. The doctor broke into a cold sweat.

Manto's story reveals what formal/academic sociology cannot. We realize what a terrible damage a politics centred on man's limited identity can do to our consciousness and praxis. How long should we play the politics of casteism, communalism and religious nationalism, and deprive us of our ability to grow, expand our horizon, and become universal? It is at this juncture that a question arises: Is *globalization* an answer? Is it encouraging us to overcome the limitedness of caste, religion, nationality, and experience what it means to be truly universal?

The kind of globalization that we experience cannot be understood without looking at the irresistible power of the market in our times—the way the market is colonizing almost everything, and you and I are being seen primarily as consumers. It may be said that till yesterday I was my caste, my religion, my nationality; but today I am what I buy and consume; I am my lifestyle, the symbols I emit, the spectacles I engage in! The overflow of commodities (material as well as symbolic) with their mythologies of 'good living', the spectacular malls promoting the belief that shopping is salvation, the credit card economy with its magical instantaneity: everything tends to make us believe that our essence lies in what we consume. It may appear that the market neutralizes the power of caste, religion, nationality. A Hindu and a Muslim in a mall look similar. When an Indian and a Pakistani buy the same gadget, eat the same fast food, and get fascinated by similar brand names, we realize that the hold of the nation-state or even religion in defining one's cultural choice is slowly eroding. It is true that secular modernity with its ethos of 'scientific reason' and 'progress' is endowed with its potential; it can lessen the influence of identities like caste and religion; it can create universal aspirations.However,the age of modernity is inseparable from the ideology of nationalism—the way the 'sovereign' nation-state demands absolute loyalty from its citizens; and, as a result, 'national identity' acquires extraordinary significance. And yes, this identity erects a wall, intensifies divisions and leads to war. Does it then mean that as the market transcends national boundaries we are moving towards oneness? Is the market a shared religion of humankind?

True, the market invades almost every sphere of life, and as technologies and media messages move faster than light, cultures overlap, and boundaries get blurred. Not solely that. What begins to emerge is hybridity. The certainty of a fixed/coherent self-identity is doubted; the solidity of caste/nationality tends to melt; or, to borrow Zygmunt Bauman's words, 'in our liquid modern times, when the free-floating, unencumbered individual is the popular hero, 'being fixed'—being 'identified'inflexibly and without retreat—gets an increasingly bad press' (Bauman 2004: 29). There is nothing stable and permanent any more; everything is in flux; everything is uncertain; things move faster than we can imagine. To refer to Bauman once again, 'today's respected authorities will be ridiculed, snubbed or despised tomorrow, celebrities will be forgotten, trend-setting idols will be remembered only in TV quizzes,...the foolproof stocks will turn into the fool's stocks, promising lifelong careers will be found to be blind alleys' (Ibid: 51). You cannot expect commitment to any particular identity.

However, it should not be forgotten that this uncertainty and hybridity may generate stress and tension. It is an experience of homelessness; it creates a need for the 'lost home'. And this quest for the 'lost home'—for regaining the 'certainties' of caste, religion, nationality—leads to yet another major trend in our times: cultural nationalism and religious fundamentalism. It seeks certainty, order, purity; it seeks to create tight boundaries; it abhors ambiguities and contradictions. No wonder, it often manifests itself through violence. The seduction of the market and the violence of religious fundamentalism; or the depthlessness of 'liquid modernity' and the rigidity of 'identity politics'—these are the two sides of the same coin. Not solely that, terrorism has begun to charaterize our world—an extremely uneven/ violent world characterized by the ethos of neo-liberalism and global capitalism. There are many ways of seeing terrorism—as nihilism, as despair, as counter-violence, as a quest for regaining the 'lost' world. But the fact is that the act of terrorism has given birth to the production of images, stereotypes, identities—terrorists belong to a particular religion, they are primarily from certain geographical localities, and they are fundamentally different from white/ liberal democrats living in the Euro-American world! Globalization as it exists is not uniting; it is dividing.

Is there a way out? Is it possible not to remain confined to one's boundaries, not to fall into the trap of militant nationalism or religious fundamentalism? Is it possible to see beyond the market—the prevailing practice of globalization, the flow of simulacra, its inherent contradictions and violence? Is it possible to have a truly authentic experience of the unity of the world, the experience of oneness through the expansion of one's heart? Is it possible to be a banyan tree—deeply rooted, yet expanding its branches into the sky? Yes, it is. But then, we need to undertake a journey—from sociology to poetry, from the outer to the inner. It is the awakening of love—the love that unites, integrates, heals, transcends boundaries. Not a confined space, but it is the infinite that becomes our aspiration, our possibility. Not surprisingly, Rabindranath Tagore—a gifted poet endowed with the spirit of religiosity as man's 'surplus', man's abundance—reminded us of this journey. He took us beyond nationalism, beyond market-driven globalization. See, for instance, Tagore's critique of the politics of nationalism. 'Nation' as a political machinery with its iron chains of organization and inflated ego obstructs the free flow of inner life of people. It is like a 'power loom' that is reckless in its operation; it breeds uniformity; it annihilates differences; it is conflict-centric. It characterizes modern Western civilization; it induces the spirit of violence. It drains man's energy from his higher nature; man's power of sacrifice is diverted from his ultimate object which is moral to the maintenance of this organization which is mechanical. Nationalism, wrote Tagore, is a great menace. He could see how 'the spectre of a new barbarity strides over Europe, teeth bare and claws unconcealed in an orgy of terror'; he could feel 'the crumbling ruins of a proud civilization lying heaped as garbage out of history' (Tagore 1961: 358). 'There was a time', Tagore said with intense pain, 'when I used to believe that the springs of a true civilization would issue out of the heart of Europe; today, as I am about to quit the world, that faith has gone bankrupt' (Ibid: 359).However, he could not afford to lose faith in man. That seemed to be the reason why he felt that 'the new dawn will come...from the East where the sun rises...' (Ibid: 359). What was unique in the East, or to put it specifically, in our civilization that we could offer to the world? Tagore felt that we should not imitate the doctrine of Western nationalism. Instead, we ought to realize that our civilization, unlike the politics of nationalism, rests on harmony; it is like an oceanic flow that accepts and integrates diverse currents. 'I have no hesitation in saying', wrote Tagore, 'that those who are gifted with the moral power of love and vision of spiritual unity...will be the fittest to take their permanent place in the age that is lying before us, and those who are constantly developing their instinct of fight and intolerance of aliens will be eliminated' (Tagore 1985: 101). As he would have said, we are required to prove our humanity through the help of our higher nature. It is precisely this freedom of soul, he felt, that our civilization celebrates. It is not the narcissism of nation-states; it is not European imperialism; it is not the utilitarianism of the market; instead, it is to see Him in everything. The greatness of man lies in uniting the finite with the infinite; and today our primary task, the poet reminded us, is precisely this *sadhana*: neither conflict nor victory, but only unity and love and ecstasy. What else could be a better illustration of this quest than Tagore's literary vision? It is in this context that I wish to refer to Gora—one of the finest characters he created in his novel, his intensity, his likes and dislikes, his love and passion, and eventually his realization of his sacred being, his freedom from limiting identities (Tagore 2011: 211-784). See the way Tagore introduced Gora. One of his college Professors used to call him the 'Snow Mountain', for he was 'outrageously white'.

Gora is six feet tall, with big bones, and fists like the paws of a tiger. The sound of his voice is deep; it is impossible to overlook him. He is the Chairman of the Hindu Patriot's Society. Hinduism fascinates him. 'Our ideas of shame or glory', he feels, 'must not depend on minute comparisons at every step with a foreign standard. We must not feel apologetic about the country of our birth—whether it be about its traditions, faith, or its scriptures—neither to others nor even to ourselves'. No wonder, Gora began religiously 'to bathe in the Ganges, regularly to perform ceremonial worship morning and evening, to take particular care of what he touched and what he ate, and even to grow a *tiki*'. He would not lose an opportunity to quarrel with an Englishman; he does not even listen to his mother Anandamoyi's appeal, and hates to eat food cooked by Christian maidservant Lachmi; he argues with his father Krishnadayal, and tries to convince him: 'If I cannot understand the deeper meaning of Hinduism today I shall do so tomorrow. Even if I cannot grasp its full significance, its path is the only one for me to pursue. The merit of some previous Hindu birth has brought me this time into a Brahmin family, and in this way, after repeated rebirths through Hindu religion and society, I shall reach my final goal'; he finds no hesitation in arguing with Paresh Babu—a calm, composed Brahmo gentlemam; he requests Sucharita—Paresh Babu's daughter (or the woman he has begun to love) : 'Come inside India, accept all her good and her evil; if there be deformity then try and cure it from within, but see it with your own eyes, understand it, think over it, turn your face towards it, become one with it. You will never understand if you stand opposed and, imbued to the bone with Christian ideas, view it from outside. Then you will only try to wound and never be of any service'. The story goes on. However, what strikes me is the turning point in Gora's life—his deep existential crisis. His father

Krishnadayal is sick; he feels like revealing what he has kept secret for years. In case Krishnadayal dies, Gora is told, he has no right to join in the funeral rites, because he is not the real son of Krishnadayal and Anandamoyi. 'It was during the Mutiny', said Krishnadayal, 'when we were at Etawa your mother, in fear of the Sepoys, took refuge one night in our house. Your father had been killed during the previous day during the fighting...He was an Irishman. That very night your mother died after giving birth to you. From that day you were brought up in our home'. Imagine its effect. 'In a single moment Gora's whole life seemed to him like some extraordinary dream. The foundations upon which, from childhood, all his life had been raised had suddenly crumbled into dust, and he was unable to understand who he was or where he stood'. But then, it was Tagore who could make it possible. The crisis brought Gora nearer to the depths of his being; he could realize the oceanic flow of love inside. How wonderful it is to hear Gora revealing this truth before Paresh Babu: 'Today I am really an Indian! In me there is no longer any opposition between Hindu, Mussulman and Christian. Today every caste in India is my caste, the food of all is my food! Today I have become so pure that I can never be afraid of contamination even in the house of the lowest of the castes. Paresh Babu, this morning, with my heart absolutely bare I have prostrated myself wholly at the knees of my India—after so long I have at length fully experienced what is meant by the mother's lap'. Gora came back, submitted before his mother. Anandamoyi lifted his head and kissed him. 'Mother, you are my mother!' exclaimed Gora. 'The mother whom I have been wandering about in search of was all the time sitting in my room at home. You have no caste, you make no distinctions, and have no hatred—you are only the image of our welfare! It is you who are India'!

## (VII)

True, living life meaningfully is to experience *love*. Love is merger; love is union; love is the art of overcoming limitedness; love is expansion; love is surrender; love is beauty, poetry, spirituality. Love is also like the elegant sunset—a truly graceful disappearance. Love is inseparable from deep melancholy. No wonder, artists, poets, mystics and all of us speak of love, strive for love. 'Drink of Love—that is life's elixir pure'—we feel like embracing Rumi for articulating what we all wanted to utter. Indeed, love has many manifestations: we love our parents, children, wives; we love our friends; we love our gods, our countries, our languages; we love nature—birds, trees, mountains, flowers. And all these forms may have diverse meanings and messages. A woman's love for her beloved has got a meaning which is qualitatively different from the way she loves her child or her father. Or, the way a nature-lover looks at the distant snow peaks is different from the way a comrade loves his political party. However, these differences notwithstanding, all experiences of love tend to converge. Because love means connectedness; love is caring, nurturing, listening. Not surprisingly, there are moments—and these moments reveal the mystery of love, its surprise, its ultimate wonder—when conventions/stereotypes collapse, and boundaries get blurred. For a man growing old, his daughter becomes his mother; for a woman, her husband becomes her child; for someone with deep pain, an enchanted tree becomes his beloved, a tree that receives his tears, and heals his wound; and it happens—although it happens rarely—when in her teacher a student finds her father, her lovely child, her spiritual companion. And most importantly at the peak moment of ecstasy even God becomes one's beloved. Imagine, for instance, that beautiful tale from the *Bhagavata Purana* (IV 1978: Ch-29). Full moon—beautiful autumn night—Krishna's melodious music. The Gopis were hypnotized. Being extremely eager to join the Lord, some who were milking cows went away leaving the milking half done; some who were serving food to the members of their family left off without serving any further; some others who were waiting upon their husbands suddenly stopped and departed. But then, Krishna asked them to return to their homes because 'it is the supreme duty of women to wait upon and render service to husbands with sincerity of hearts, to look after the well-being of relatives and to nourish children'. However, they were reluctant to go back; instead, they appealed: 'Please do not abandon us. For when you, the eternally dear Lord are available, what purpose can be served by husbands, sons and other relatives who are nothing but a source of trouble. Therefore, be pleased to be gracious to us, oh Lotus-eyed God! Extinguish, Oh darling, with the flood of the nectar of Your lips the conflagration of passion set ablaze in our hearts by you, with your beguiling smiles, side glances and melodious music, otherwise, with our bodies consumed by the fire of separation, we shall, by meditating upon you, attain to the position of your feet'. And then, listening to the prayer of the Gopis, Krishna conferred bliss on them; surrounded by them, he entered the cool sandy bed of the river, and sported with them. By stretching out his arms, embracing them, touching their hands, locks of hair, thighs, waists, bosom, by indulging in jokes and by pricking them gently with his nails, by his sportive glances and smiles, Krishna gave delight to the Gopis.

Indeed, with love everything around us begins to get enchanted. The tree whispers, you look at the sky, and in those stars you find all your loved ones you met in your previous lives. Love does not limit itself. Love crosses limits. Love overflows. No wonder, love is also melancholic; to love is to die; to love is to feel the pain of separation. 'My heart left me', as Amir Khusrau expressed the voice of every lover, 'but longing for you won't leave my heart. My heart broke apart, but pain for you won't diminish' (Khusrau 201: 34). Indeed, love is surrender—the withering away of the narcissistic ego. This is like the river merging into the ocean. That is why, love is beyond victory and defeat, success and failure. It reaffirms itself in the relational self that is vast and infinite. It is in this context that I wish to invoke *Kabuliwalla* (The pedlar from Kabul)—an extraordinary character that Tagore created in one of his path-breaking short stories (Tagore in Chattopadhyay 2010: 56-66). See the way his relationship with Mini—a five-year-old girl evolved. One day Mini saw him. 'In dirty baggy clothes, a long sack hanging from his shoulder and three or four packets of grapes in his hand a Kabuliwalla was ambling down the road.' Mini was amazed and excited; she began to call loudly; 'Kabuliwalla, O Kabuliwalla'. But 'as soon as he turned his face with a smile and began to approach our house, she ran off and vanished.' Possibly 'she had a sort of ingrained belief that a search in his sack might produce one or two human beings like her'. However, Kabuliwalla was irresistible; Mini was destined to be close to him. At this juncture, Tagore as a storyteller expressed his wonder. 'A few days later, one morning as I was going out on some work, I found that my daughter, sitting on the bench near the door, was talking incessantly, while the Kabuliwalla sat at her feet listening with an encouraging smile and at times in proper contexts throwing in his own comments in his hybrid Bengali'. Indeed, Mini had never found such a patient audience in anyone except her father. What a marvellous bond! Rahamat—which was the pedlar's name—had visited her almost daily, and by bringing her goodies, had infiltrated far into her greedy little heart. The day he failed to come in the morning, he turned up in the evening. 'When Mini came running with a smile on her face and 'Kabuliwalla, O Kabuliwalla' on her lips, two friends of unequal ages sharing their old artless jokes, all one's heart filled with a sense of contentment'. However, there was a turning point. Someone owed Rahamat some money for a shawl; he had fraudulently denied the debt; a brawl ensued and eventually Rahamat had stabbed him with the dagger. He got several years of prison. So many years had passed by; Kabuliwalla was almost forgotten; Mini was no longer a little girl; her marriage was settled. It was her marriage day—a beautiful autumn morning; there was great hustle and bustle in the house; guests were coming in; *shehnai* was plying since early morning. And then, all of a sudden, as life is never tired of surprising us, emerged Rahamat—Mimi's Kabuliwalla.It was an auspicious day; a murderer's presence might destroy the sanctity of the occasion; and hence Mini's father told him: 'Today we have an occasion in the house; I am rather busy. You had better go'. He was about to leave; yet with some hesitation he expressed his desire to meet Mini. He had even brought a box of grapes besides some raisins and almonds in a paper packet commemorating their old friendship. 'I had brought those fruits for the girl', he said, 'Please pass them on to her'. After taking them, as Mini's father was about to pay him, he appealed: 'Please do not give me any money. As you have a daughter, so do I in my home. Only recalling her face do I bring some titbits when I come to your daughter, certainly not to trade'. And then he showed the imprint of a little palm—not a photograph, not an oil painting, just his daughter's palm smeared with lampblack and pressed on to the paper. This little momento he carried close to his heart as he came every year to Calcutta peddling fruits on its streets. It was a moment of awakening. Tagore as a story-teller presenting himself as Mini's father described the moment with heightened sensitivity: 'Traces of tears appeared at the corners of my eyes. The moment obliterated the fact that he was an Afghan fruit seller and I a respectable Bengali Babu. It was a moment of realization: what he was at bottom, the same was I; I was a father, so was he. The hand impression of his mountain-dwelling little daughter reminded me of my own Mini'. Yes, Mini—draped in a red silk sari, her brow patterned with sandal paste—met him; it was not easy to resume their old friendship. Possibly he realized that his own daughter too had meanwhile become as grown-up as Mini; with her as well he would have to pick up a fresh thread of conversation. 'In the morning under the balmy autumn sun, while the *shehnai* kept pouring out its strains, Rahamat sat in an alley of Calcutta brooding over a desert hill of Afghanistan'.

Boundless love and smiles and tears! But then, why is it that we find ourselves in a world filled with violence and hatred, envy and possessiveness, fragmentation and finitude? One main reason is our ego—its urge to conquer and possess. It is afraid of giving, melting, dissolving. Because of this armour called 'ego' love degenerates; the 'beloved' becomes a piece of possession—a bundle of desires and expectations. Love loses its spirit; societal rigidity and excessive routinization kill it, its mysterious flow. No wonder, even marriage, for many, becomes a compulsion, a habit; it loses the spiritual ecstasy that connects the two with the cosmos; instead, it gets reduced into a series of routinized acts—cooking, eating, saving, insuring, investing, rearing children and even making love! With this begins fear, insecurity and violence. We restrict the flow of love; we erect walls, create rigid structures and boundaries. And hence we see a series of contradictions and paradoxes. While a mother is intensely caring for her own child, she may remain utterly indifferent to others. Or, how often because of the narcissistic ego of the nation-state, loving our own country becomes equivalent to hating the 'enemy' nations. Love gets fragmented; far from uniting, it begins to exclude, separate and divide. Casteism, militant nationalism, racism, terrible family pride—these are nothing but the tragic fate of love getting transformed into its opposite.True, love concretizes itself in deeply intimate personal relationships. In your beloved, your friend, your child you find the container of all that you have: your affections, your love, your prayer, your positive aspirations. But then, there are moments of awakening when you realize that love overflows; the embodied form of love is essentially an articulation of the infinite; to love someone is to feel connected with everyone—the way Tagore's Kabuliwalla, precisely because of his love for his own daughter in Afghanistan, became intensely connected with Mini—a little girl from Calcutta. This is the supreme realization of love. And hence to dissociate love from devotion and prayer is to restrain its flow; and then ironically, love and hatred go together.

Is it our destiny? Or, is it possible to overcome egotistic pride and possessiveness, and experience love as an oceanic flow, and feel the beloved in every creation? It may be argued that our earthly/material existence has not yet been able to elevate itself to such a higher stage. Yet, despite Freud and Nietzsche, Hobbes and Spencer, there is a deep-rooted longing for love, merger and surrender; we continue to be charmed by Jesus, his revealing message: "You have heard that it was said, 'Love your neighbour and hate your enemy'. But I tell you: Love your enemies and pray for those who persecute you that you may be sons of your Father in heaven...If you love those who love you, what reward will you get? Are not even the tax collectors doing that? And if you greet only your brothers, what are you doing more than others? Do not even pagans do that? Be perfect, therefore, as your heavenly Father is perfect." Likewise, we like to believe that one day we would all find ourselves in a world in which everyone becomes a Sufi; a world where love is a flow; love is natural, spontaneous, love is in abundance; a world where, to quote Jalaluddin Rumi, 'Love is the barometer of God's mystery in our hearts. Love, whether it be of this world or the other, leads us to the Lord who is the Lord of all!' (Jamal 2009: 145).

It may be said that no reflection on the miraculous power of love remains complete without referring to the man-woman relationship—particularly, its sexual/erotic component. Enough has already been said and written about sexuality: how it has inspired poets and artists, aroused the analytical skill of psychoanalysts, and caused a note of concern for the 'protectors' of social order. The sexual energy is rooted in the facticity of our existence; negating it is like negating a very real/important aspect of human life; and its consequences, as Sigmund Freud wanted us to believe, could prove to be disastrous leading to nervous and mental diseases. Society, in the name of its civilizational ideal and moral order, seeks to deny the importance of sexuality, its instinctual impulses. In one of his lectures Freud asserted: 'Society believes that no greater threat to its civilization could arise than if the sexual instincts were to be liberated and returned to their original aims...It has no interest in the recognition of the strength of the sexual instincts or in the demonstration of the importance of sexual life to the individual. On the contrary, with an educational aim in view, it has set about diverting attention from that whole field of ideas. That is why it will not tolerate this outcome of psychoanalytic research and far prefers to stamp it as something aesthetically repulsive and morally reprehensible, or as something dangerous' (Freud 1981: 48). However, Freud was determined to awaken us of the importance of the sexual life of human beings. He broadened the notion of sexuality. For him, as he spoke in another lecture, it is not just about 'normal' adult sexuality: an activity which is concerned with the bodily pleasure, and in particular 'with the sexual organs of the opposite sex, and which in the last resort aims at the union of the genitals and the performance of the sexual act' (Ibid: 344); instead, sexuality manifests itself in multiple and diverse ways. In fact, what distinguished Freud was his emphasis on infantile sexuality. 'To suppose that children have no sexual life...but suddenly acquire it between the ages of twelve and fourteen', said Freud, 'would be as improbable, and indeed senseless, biologically as to suppose that they brought no genitals with them into the world and only grew them only at time of puberty' (Ibid: 353). Imagine that blissful sight: a child falling asleep after being sated at his mother's breast. It is not just a nutritive instinct. Bacause the fact is that even when the infant does not demand further food, he continues to suck his mother's breast; and, as Freud said, 'soon things come to a point at which he cannot go to sleep without having sucked' (Ibid: 355). Indeed, this expression of blissful satisfaction will be repeated later in life after the experience of a sexual orgasm. 'Sucking at the mother's breast is the starting-point of the whole of sexual life'; no wonder, said Freud, 'if an infant could speak, he would no doubt pronounce the act of sucking at his mother's breast by far the most important in his life' (Ibid: 356). In other words, sexuality manifests itself also through the 'erotogenic zones' like the mouth and lips. In fact, as it is argued, man's sexual life passes through a series of stages—from this 'oral' stage to the 'anal' stage (we are told that infants have feelings of pleasure in the process of evacuating urine and faeces and they soon arrange those actions in such a way as to bring them the greatest possible pleasure through the corresponding excitations of the erotogenic zones of the mucous membrane) to the 'phallic' stage to the 'latency' period to what is regarded as the normal 'genital' stage. The roots of 'abnormal' sexuality—all sorts of perversions, Freud asserted boldly, lie in some sort of fixation to the early stage of infantile sexuality. Quite often repression—or, increased difficulty in obtaining normal sexual satisfaction in real life—brings out 'perversions' which must have been present in them in a latent form. And there seems to be no escape from repression. Society seeks to tame and restrict the sexual instinct; otherwise, 'the instinct would break every dam and wash away the laboriously erected work of civilization' (Ibid: 353). As it is argued, society does not have enough provisions to keep its members alive unless they work, and hence it must divert their energies from sexual activity to work. Those who cannot bear the burden of repression tend to become neurotic. In yet another important lecture Freud said, neurotic symptoms serve for the patients' sexual satisfaction; 'they are a substitute for satisfaction of this kind, which the patients are without in their lives' (Ibid: 340). People fall sick, become neurotic, develop symptoms, or express all sorts of 'perversions'. But then, Freud saw another possibility—the process of 'sublimation' through which sexual impulses are 'diverted from their sexual aims and directed to others that are socially higher and no longer sexual' (Ibid: 47-48). It is in this context that his classical work on Leonardo da Vinci acquires relevance. I just wish to refer to his reflections on Leonardo's celebrated painting: Mona Lisa. In Mona Lisa's magical smile Freud saw two distinct elements—'the most perfect representation of the contrasts which dominate the erotic life of women; the contrast between reserve and seduction, and between the most devoted tenderness and a sensuality that is ruthlessly demanding—consuming men as if they were alien beings' (Freud 2002). Did this smile lie dormant in his mind as an old memory? Look at Leonardo's illegitimate birth, his early childhood. He spent the critical first years of his life with his poor, forsaken mother. And it was quite likely, as Freud imagined, that 'in her love for child the poor forsaken mother had to give vent to all her memories of the caresses he had enjoyed as well as her longing for new ones; and she was forced to do so not only to compensate herself for having no husband, but also to compensate her for having no father to fondle him; and so, like all unsatisfied mothers, she took her little son in place of her husband, and by the too early maturing of his eroticism robbed him of a part of his masculinity' (Ibid: 73). Was it the reason that Leonardo could never be able to come out of his attachment to his mother? Was it not surprising that he represented the 'cool repudiation of sexuality—a thing that would scarcely be expected of an artist and a portrayer of feminine beauty' (Ibid: 15)? As we are told, 'it is doubtful whether Leonardo ever embraced a woman in passion; nor is it known that he had any intimate mental relationship with a woman' (Ibid: 17). Possibly 'he had for long been under the dominance of an inhibition which forbade him ever again to desire such caresses from the lips of women' (Ibid: 73). He sublimated this urge, and as a painter strove to reproduce the smile with his brush; 'it is possible that Leonardo has denied the unhappiness of his erotic life and has triumphed over it in his art, by representing the wishes of the boy infatuated with his mother' (Ibid: 74).

Here my concern is not to celebrate Freud's overemphasis on sexuality; this is only to prepare ourselves to understand the nuances of the role of sexuality in human life. Let us accept the fact that sexuality, because of its very power, causes concern; not everyone, it is feared, is capable of handling it. How can we forget that the same sexual energy, if not communicated in a truly relational/dialogic/egalitarian mode, becomes utterly violent—a ruthless process of objectification of human relationships, manipulation of people for immediate self-gratification, and assertion of power? The commodification of women, the pornographic mindset, the sexualization of goods, commodities and services—we find ourselves in a culture that, far from softening and humanizing sexuality, uses it for purely instrumental purposes. It would not be wrong to say that what goes on in the name of 'popular culture'—songs, ads, television visuals, gossip columns in glossy magazines—further cultivates this mindset. Sexual abuse or rape, it seems, is the cumulative effect of this process. No wonder, there is also an attempt to control sexuality. The 'protectors' of culture and morality speak of censorship; parents feel shy of discussing sexuality with children. This taboo, paradoxically, further exaggerates the interest in sexuality leading to multiple aberrations.

There is yet another important dimension to this discourse that we need to reflect on. For some, particularly ascetics and saints, sexuality is seen as a hindrance, an obstacle to man's spiritual growth. A sexual relationship, it is feared, diverts the seeker of truth; and hence we come across innumerable tales/illustrations from religious mythologies that remind us of this danger. It is in this context that we can see how women, despite their association with benevolence and motherhood, are also seen to be erotic—full of sexuality and desire—diverting the seekers from the single-minded devotion to truth.This dark imagery, as Sudhir Kakar pointed out, breaks through such proverbs as, 'Fire is never satisfied with fuel, the ocean is never filled with the rivers, death is never satisfied by living beings and women are never satisfied with men' ( Kakar 1982: 93). Realizing spiritual truth is like overcoming these obstacles, these temptations of *kama*, desire and flesh! However, it is not easy. We should not forget that in mythology, when Shiva destroys Kama, the god of sexual desire, Kama's essence enters the limbs of Devi, the great mother-goddess and archetypal woman. In our times, a man like Mohandas Karamchand Gandhi, to take a striking example, sought to undertake this journey. Gandhi's 'confessions' reveal how sexuality continued to bother him;

his early encounter with a prostitute and resultant shame and guilt; his lust and passion for Kasturba and hence his failure to remain with his father at the time of his departure from the world; his repeated failures to practise the vow of *brahmacharya*; and at the last stage of his illustrious life-trajectory his 'experiments' (sleeping naked with women in order to test his celibacy)— everything seems to indicate how uneasy he was with sexuality, how he sought to control it, sublimate it. As Gandhi said, it was in South Africa that he began seriously to think of taking the *brahmacharya* vow; he began to realize the importance of observing *brahmacharya* even with respect to his wife. Here he made an interesting observation. 'So long as I was the slave of my lust, my faithfulness was worth nothing. To be fair to my wife, I must say that she was never the temptress. It was therefore the easiest thing for me to take the vow of *brahmacharya,* if only I willed it. It was my weak will or lustful attachment that was the obstacle' (Gandhi 1976: 154). Indeed, it was not easy. 'Even after my conscience had been roused in the matter', he did not hesitate to confess, ' I failed twice' (Ibid: 154). In fact, it was only in 1906 that the final resolution could be made; 'the idea flashed upon me that if I wanted to devote myself to the service of the community, I must relinquish the desire for children and wealth and live the life of a *vanaprastha*—of one retired from household cares' (Ibid: 155). Although it was a matter of 'ever-increasing joy' (in terms of the 'protection of the body, the mind, and the soul'), it was by no means an easy task. 'Even though I am past fifty-six years', wrote Gandhi, 'I realize how hard a thing it is. Every day I realize more and more that it is like walking on the sword's edge, and I see every moment the necessity for eternal vigilance' (Ibid: 156). Was it the reason that Gandhi tried to test his capacity time and again? At a time when there was widespread violence in Calcutta and Noakhali, Bihar and Delhi (1946-1948), Gandhi was passing through severe moral crisis; it was quite likely that he felt the need for examining his own being, his 'purity' and *brahmacharya*. After all, for him, in order to be a fitter instrument of human service, the sensual aspects of his being had to be brought under full restraint. At this juncture, he started sleeping with a young girl in order to prove his celibacy; an 'experiment' of this kind was not appreciated by many of his admirers. In one of his letters to Satish Chandra Mukherji of Banaras, Gandhi wrote: 'A young girl (19) who is in the place of granddaughter to me by relation shares the same bed with me, not for any animal satisfaction but for valid moral reasons. She claims to be free from the passion that a girl of her age generally has and I claim to be a practised *brahmachari*. Do you see anything bad or unjustifiable in this juxtaposition? I ask this question because some of my intimate associates hold it to be wholly unjustified and even a breach of *brahmacharya*. I hold a totally opposite view' (Quoted in Bose 1974: 134).

Here my intention is not to become judgemental about Gandhi's 'experiments'; nor am I capable of evaluating the meaning or necessity of his fascination with *brahmacharya*. What I, however, wish to add is that while sexuality generates mixed feelings, there is no reason to be excessively fearful about it. Because when sexuality is communicative, not instrumental; when it is a union of the spirits, it becomes deeply humane and sacred. It loses its aggression; instead, it emerges as the fragrance of a flower. The body becomes a carrier of the spirit through which the flame of love illumines the lover and the beloved. It takes the man-woman relationship to a great height; God becomes intimate; divinity is felt through the whisper and music of human bodies. In this context it would not be inappropriate to refer to the dalliance of Sati and Siva as described in the *Siva Purana* (In Shastri Vol. I 1970: 369). See the way Siva sported with her. Sometimes he would be sporting with her earrings, tying and untying; sometimes he would take the necklace off her breasts and press them with his hands; sometimes he would gather lotuses and other beautiful flowers and decorate her with them as though with ornaments. In other words, deep love (not lust, not instrumental urge to possess one's body) makes a sexual union rhythmic and enchanting. That is why, the answer, like all good answers, is an awareness, a sensitivity, a willingness to experience life in its totality.

At this juncture, there is yet another important question that haunts us. Is love possible if men and women are situated in asymmetrical power relations? We know how patriarchy seeks to erect hierarchical dualities, how it privileges men, and makes it possible for them to have control over women—their bodies and minds, their modes of living and seeing the world. Its consequences are disastrous; it negates the flow of love. See the way it dehumanizes men. The 'masculinity' they adore—a ruthlessly competitive man earning, fulfilling his woman's 'needs', protecting her 'honour', or asserting their power in 'conquering' women—is filled with the burden of ego; it cannot melt, it cannot surrender, it cannot shed tears. Patriarchy is powerful because even women, barring exceptions, tend to internalize its logic, and thereby normalize it. The 'femininity' they tend to glamorize—a woman with 'softness' and 'beauty' always willing to be protected and pampered by her man—does by no means glorify womanhood; instead, it is like reducing oneself into a doll; it is like encouraging one's own objectification; it is the negation of love. Who knows it more than Henrik Ibsen's Nora? Eight years of marriage, and eventually she realizes that she is living in a 'doll's house'. See her pain and resultant awakening. She finds her voice, and makes it clear before her husband: 'When I was at home with papa, he told me his opinion about everything, and so I had the same opinions; and if I differed from him I concealed the fact, because he would not have liked it. He called me his doll-child, and he played with me just as I used to play with my dolls. And when I came to live with you I was simply transferred from papa's hands into yours. You arranged everything according to your own taste, and so I got the same tastes as you—or else I pretended to, I am really not quite sure which—I think sometimes the one and sometimes the other. When I look back on it, it seems to me as if I had been living here like a poor woman—just from hand to mouth...You and papa have committed a great sin against me...No, I have never been happy. I thought I was, but it has never really been so' (Ibsen 2005: 89-90).

How is it possible to love a woman, and at the same time reduce her into an object of possession? Or, for that matter, how is it possible to love a man, and at the same time reduce him into a 'resource' to be measured in terms of money and status? In patriarchy love is not love; it is violence; it is a broken/distorted communication; it enhances men's narcissistic ego and women's pathetic dependence. But the strength and purity of love, we should not forget, lies in its ability to overcome this dualistic opposition between 'masculinity' and 'femininity'. In that authentic experience of love, a true lover knows, the narcissistic ego of man withers away; man fulfils himself in surrendering before its flow; and the 'passivity' of femininity is felt as the sound of the universe, a woman becomes the light that heals, generates wisdom and illumines man. Perhaps the experience of love is the only answer to a ruthlessly patriarchal machine of life-negating/instrumental culture. Not surprisingly then, Tagore with his vision could imagine a character like Nandini in his play *Red Oleanders*. Nandini as resistance is filled with love and music; Nandini is inner conscience; Nandini is what patriarchy has forgotten; Nandini is the eternal feminine that seeks to see beyond the greedy hyper-masculinist machine. 'The world', wrote Tagore, 'has become the world of Jack and Giant—the Giant who is not a gigantic man, but a multitude of men turned into a gigantic system' (Tagore 1925: 283-85). In such a world which has 'no serenity of soul to realize and enjoy', Tagore introduced Nandini—the heroine of the play. She is a 'real woman who knows that wealth and power are *maya*, and that the highest expression of life is in love'. Tagore hoped that this 'treasure-house' in woman's heart would enable her to 'restore the human to the desolated world of man'. 'The joy of this faith', the poet articulated with absolute clarity, 'has inspired me to pour all my heart into painting against the background of black shadows—the nightmare of a devil's temptation—the portrait of Nandini as the bearer of the message of reality, the saviour through death'.

## (VIII)

We seek to enter the realm of love—the domain of poetic vision and imagination. However, it may be accused that we are not speaking the language of science—the language of *reason*. Scientific reason, it is said, objectifies the world as it is with all its hard facts; it has got nothing to do with the romance of a poet! In fact, an archetypal modern citizen is one who loves science, gets thrilled at its spectacular technology, prefers to apply 'scientific method' in every domain of enquiry, and hence avoids what cannot be explained through the categories of analytical reason. No wonder, it begins with doubt; it doubts everything. Recall Rene Descartes's *Meditations of First Philosophy*. 'I was convinced', as he wrote, 'that I must once for all seriously undertake to rid myself of all the opinions which I had formerly accepted'. He began to doubt all that he had learned from the senses or through the senses. For example, 'there is the fact that I am here, seated by the fire, attired in a dressing gown, having this paper in my hand and other similar matters'; but then, 'how often it has happened to me that in the night I dreamt that I found myself in this particular place, that I was dressed and seated near the fire, whilst in reality I was lying undressed in bed'! There are no certain indications, as Descartes would argue, by which we may clearly distinguish wakefulness from sleep. There seemed to be no end to this indulgence with doubt. He went to such an extent as to feel: 'I shall consider myself having no hands, no eyes, no flesh, no blood, nor any senses, yet falsely believing myself to possess all these things'. See the effect of this doubt. 'There is some deceiver, very powerful and very cunning who even employs his ingenuity in deceiving me', he felt. However, amidst this doubt, he was trying to find some certainty—a 'firm and permanent structure in the sciences'. One can deceive you only if you exist. The fact that one is being deceived makes it certain that one exists.'Without doubt I exist also if he deceives me...I am, I exist is necessarily true each time that I pronounce it, or that I mentally conceive it'. But then,who is this 'I'? For Descartes, one cannot be equated with one's senses, one's body. Because these are sources of error and deception. Even as far as the most intimate and internal experience like pain is concerned, one can be deceived. 'I have learned from some persons whose arms or legs have been cut off, that they seemed to feel pain in that part which had been amputated'. No wonder, he destroyed all the faith which he had rested in his senses. Moreover, as we are told, there is a great difference between the mind and body; whereas the body is by nature always divisible, the mind is entirely indivisible. For example, 'if a foot, or an arm, or some other part is separated from my body, I am aware that nothing has been taken away from my mind'. In contrast, as he added, 'when I consider the mind, I cannot distinguish in myself any parts, but apprehend myself to be clearly one and entire'. That is why, he placed supreme emphasis on the mind or thinking which, as it was argued, is entirely and absolutely distinct from the body, and can exist without it. 'Thought', Descartes asserted, 'is an attribute that belongs to me; it cannot be separated from me. I am a thing which thinks, doubts, understands, affirms, denies, wills, refuses...'.

Yes, this rational thinking—abstract, disembodied, dispassionate thinking, thinking not contaminated by the senses of pleasure and pain—is indeed an important faculty of cognition and comprehension; it does play an important role in one's life, in the development of modern science and technology. Yet, it is equally important to remember that man is not just rational; abstract thought alone is not his essence; he is also a dreamer; his imagination, his intuition, his feeling, his ecstasy are no less important than what Descartes would have regarded as rational thought. Furthermore, the same reason, if not softened by the touch of love, becomes instrumental; dualism—reason vs. intuition, thinking vs. feeling, objective vs. subjective, masculine vs. femininine—is inherently violent. Imagine the effect of this violent/instrumentral reason. Its detachment, its distance, the wall it erects between the knower and the known, its cold cognition, its rigorous measurement and calculation—everything leads to the principle of domination and control. Nature loses its mystery, gets despiritualized; the tree does not whisper any more; the river does not philosophize; the moon does not evoke poetry; instead, everything has to be 'known', reduced into a 'resource' in order to be conquered—for electricity, for newsprints, for furniture, for space research, for national pride. It is, therefore, not surprising that there are critics who argue that modernity is no longer liberating; technology itself is domination; violence is implicit in the way it has overemphasized instrumentral rationality. And this violence severely affects human relationships. We are now buyers and sellers, professionals and clients; and in this engagement there is no ecstasy, no warmth; there is only a principle of calculation—give and take! Furthermore, the state, its bureaucracy, its surveillance machinery uses this instrumental reason for collecting all sorts of data and information about people in order to administer, discipline and control them. In other words, this sort of reason negates love, understanding and empathy. Not surprisingly, Zygmunt Bauman would tell us that the Holocaust, far from being an aberration, was an inevitable outcome of modernity—its bureaucratic impersonality, its techno-scientific/instrumental orientation to life (Bauman 1989). Indeed, what was witnessed was nothing less than a massive scale of 'social engineering'. After all, the chimneys—the very symbol of the modern factory system—poured forth acrid smoke produced by burning human flesh; the brilliantly organized railroad grid of modern Europe carried a new kind of raw material to the factories; in the gas chambers the victims inhaled noxius gas generated by the advanced chemical industry of Germany; engineers designed the crematoria; and the end product (meaning death) was marked carefully on the manager's production charts. To quote Bauman, 'we live in a type of society that made the Holocaust possible, and that contained nothing which could stop the Holocaust from happening' (Ibid: 88). For the technical success of bureaucratic operations all moral standards were considered irrelevant; 'organizational discipline' was substituted for moral responsibility; and phrases like the 'sanctity of human life' sounded alien. Moreover, as Bauman did not forget us to remind, 'modern genocide is a gardener's job' (Ibid: 92). And who does not know that there are weeds wherever there is a garden, and hence weeds are to be eliminated? Like weeds Hitler's victims were eliminated/killed because they did not fit, for one reason or another, the scheme of a gardener's vision of a perfect society. It was, therefore, seen as a creative, not a destructive activity! Indeed, the Holocaust showed 'what the rationalizing, designing, controlling dreams and efforts of modern civilization are able to accomplish if not mitigated, curbed or counteracted' (Ibid: 93). Even science, it should not be forgotten, cleared the way to genocide. Bauman's observations were indeed penetrating: 'As values and norms had been proclaimed immanently and irreparably subjective, instrumentality was left as the only field where the search for excellence was feasible. Science wanted to be value-free and took pride in being such. By institutional pressure and by ridicule, it silenced the preachers of morality. In the process, it made itself morally blind and speechless. It dismantled all the barriers that could stop it from cooperating...in designing the most effective and rapid methods of...mass killing' (Ibid: 108-09).

The tyranny of reason has caused pain; it subdues other voices; it confines and insulates what it categorizes as madness. 'We have yet to write the history of that other form of madness', said Michel Foucault with such great insight, 'by which men, in an act of sovereign reason, confine their neighbours, and communicate and recognize each other through the merciless language of non-madness' ( Quoted in Sheridan 1980: 13). The tyranny of reason legitimated by Newtonian physics and Cartesian rationalism insulates everything that constitutes a threat to its rule. Madness is, therefore, a judgement—a judgement passed by one part of the human mind on another. Reason fails to listen to those labelled 'mad'. Not surprisingly, 'the language of psychiatry, which is a monologue of reason about madness, could be established only on the basis of such a silence' (Ibid: 14). It should not be forgotten that before the advent of modern rationalism and science, Reason and Madness were not relegated to separate, non-communicating cells. I wish to draw insights from Foucault, and see how before the mid-17th century the connotation of 'folly' as used in literature and art conveyed a meaning different from what we regard as 'madness' in our times. Yes, King Lear is folly; but majesty does fall to folly, and in folly Lear finds the wisdom he never knew as king. However, after the mid-17th century folly/madness and its free communication with Reason began to disappear. After all, for Descartes—the doubting philosopher—madness meant dreams and all forms of error. The consequences were obvious: the exclusion of madness from the centre of intellectual life, and its demotion to the purely negative, dependent status of reason. With absolute brilliance Foucault narrated this entire history of exclusion—from the birth of the asylum to the hegemony of psychiatry and its language of Reason. When the discourse of mental illness is all-pervading, there is no communication with the mad man. Instead, as Foucault observed, 'the man of reason delegates the physician to madness, thereby authorizing reason only through the abstract universality of disease'; and, as he added, 'the man of madness communicates with society only by the intermediary of an equally abstract reason which is order, physical and moral constraint, the anonymous pressure of the group, the requirements of conformity' (Ibid: 14-15). This does by no means demonstrate love, empathy and communication. No wonder, Foucault did not forget to remind us of Dostoyevsky's prophetic message: 'It is not by confining one's neighbours that one is convinced of one's own sanity'.

Apart from these discontents, it is equally important to acknowledge how this one-sided emphasis on Reason tends to make us insensitive to the other faculties of knowledge. Take, for instance, *intuition*. It overcomes the limits imposed by empiricism and rationality, and hence as a flash of truth, it illumines, awakens and makes us see the invisible, feel its wonder and magic, and experience the transcendental. It is this intuition that enables a poet to see eternity in a handful of sand; it enables a singer to find profound music in the way an old leaf falls down from the tree; it becomes possible for the mystic to transform the mundane into the sacred; and a devotee experiences human love as a communion with the divine. Life without this intuition is dull; it may have comforts—the comforts provided by the spectacular success of science, technology and commerce; but it would be devoid of inspiration and wonder.

Those who feel it enter the domain of *faith*. Yes, I call it faith—faith not in the sense of blind acceptance, an imposition from above, from the priestcraft, from the officialdom; but faith emanating from deep realization, from that flash of truth that intuition makes one face to face with. I feel inspired to refer to Swami Vivekananda's meeting with Ramakrishna—his Master. Yes, Ramakrishna looked like an ordinary man, with nothing remarkable about him. And Vivekananda came from the university town which, he felt, was sending out 'sceptics and materialists by the hundreds every year'. So he doubted: 'Can this man be a great teacher'? This led him to ask the question: 'Do you believe in God, Sir'? 'Yes. Because I see Him just as I see you here, only in a much intenser sense' (Vivekananda, Vol. IV 1989: 179), replied the Master. See its impact. Something happened; it was a flash of truth; it altered Vivekananda's way of seeing: 'For the first time I found a man who dared to say that he saw God, that religion was a reality to be felt, to be sensed in an infinitely more intense way than we can sense the world. I began to go to that man, day after day, and I actually saw that religion could be given. One touch, one glance can change a whole life. I have read about Buddha and Christ and Muhammad, about all those different luminaries of ancient times, how they would stand up and say, 'Be thou whole', and the man became whole. I now found it to be true, and when I myself saw this man, all scepticism was brushed aside' (Ibid: 179). Likewise, as I look at Sri Aurobindo's Uttarpara Speech (Aurobindo 1972: 1-10), I see how the deep intuitive insight altered him, showed him his path, and took him from politics to spirituality. It was in the jail that he began to see Sri Krishna. 'I looked at the jail that secluded me from men and it was no longer by its high walls that I was imprisoned; no, it was Vasudeva who surrounded me. I walked under the branches of the tree, I knew it was Vasudeva, it was Sri Krishna whom I saw standing there and holding over me his shade' (Ibid: 4 ). Sri Aurobindo spoke of the impact of this deeper vision. He kept listening to the voice within: 'I am guiding, therefore fear not. Turn to your own work for which I have brought you to jail and when you come out, remember never to fear, never to hesitate...Whatever clouds may come, whatever dangers and sufferings, whatever difficulties, whatever impossibilities, there is nothing impossible, nothing difficult' (Ibid: 6). It is this intuition—or, this close intimacy with truth, the awakening of the inner voice—that makes such a fundamental difference. No matter how many radical books you have read, how many party conferences you have attended, how many political demonstrations you have joined, you cannot have authentic faith in socialism unless—even in this empirically valid bourgeois civilization—you have seen yourself in others, and felt immense joy in coming out of your atomized existence. Likewise, even if you have followed religious leaders, practised all sorts of rituals, read scriptures, you won't have real faith in a power that transcends finitude and limitations, if you have not got the glimpses of the Energy that spreads out, infuses everything, radiates love and generates a profound sense of oneness. Reason divides; it operationalizes, dissects, analyzes; it causes doubt. But it is intuition that heals, unites and integrates. It is this faith based on intuition, experience and deep realization that makes one jump into the domain of the invisible. And I would argue that authentic religiosity or spirituality emanates from this faith, intuition, love and receptivity.

This is not to negate reason. This is only to suggest that we need to move beyond reason. We have our finite existence; yet, we seek infinity. We live in time; yet we strive for eternity. It is this constant mediation between time and timelessness, history and eternity, form and formlessness, finite and infinite, earth and sky that takes us to the domain of true religiosity and spirituality. It is in this context that we need to rethink education. We know that in our times to be 'educated' means to master what formal educational institutions regard as 'legitimate' knowledge. With secularization, rationalization and scientific revolution, as we see, legitimate knowledge is often seen to be secular, scientific and technical. The process of acquiring this knowledge is accomplished through diverse practices—intellectual cognition, memorization of hard facts, interpretation of codified texts, evolving the skill of speaking/writing a specialized language... And there is a scale that measures the level of one's educational achievement—from a school drop out to a Ph.D holder. Despite its many achievements—for example, creation of experts for doing technical/professional jobs, or development of a massive techno-scientific infrastructure, this sort of education exists purely in the material-secular domain; reason is its base, information is its sign, intellect is its pride; it fails to have a contact with the transcendental, the invisible; it is devoid of love and faith. It has got its prose, but not poetry; it has got its practical achievement, but not the ecstasy of dance; it has got its economics, but not music. No wonder, we have amidst us superbly intelligent economists and financial experts promoting the sale of junk food, pesticides, lavish consumer items; we have university educated defence experts adding to the narcissism of the nation-state, promoting the manufacturing of destructive weapons. Educated people engage in war, petty politics; educated people rape, murder, kill; educated people loot, accumulate, possess inexplicable wealth!

We, therefore, need a shift: from a system of education based on mere intellectual cognition and accumulation of information to a rhythm of awakening of our innate possibilities that generate waves of love, harmony and connectedness. This is not to deny reason. This is not to deny information. This is to see beyond, and realize what connects us with everything—old people with wrinkled faces playing with their grandchildren, those tiny flowers attracting colourful butterflies, the ocean responding to the radiant moon, birds coming back and taking shelter in the banyan tree. In a beautiful act of communication Jiddu Krishnamurti once reminded schoolchildren: 'Education is not just to pass examinations, take a degree and a job, get married and settle down, but also to be able to listen to the birds, to see the sky, to see the extraordinary beauty of a tree, and the shape of the hills, and to feel with them, to be really, directly in touch with them' (Krishnamurti 2006: 8). He made us confront a pertinent question: Why are we being educated? Is it only for being excellent in mathematics, geography and history, and to conform, to fit into the stream of social and economic activity? 'We have come to a point in history', Krishnamurti added, 'where we have to create a new culture, a totally different kind of existence, not based on consumerism and industrialism, but a culture based on a real quality of religion' (Ibid: 11). But the question is: What is this real quality of religion? It has got nothing to do with labels, with ritualism, with dogmas. Instead, here is a movement towards aesthetics, towards the treasure of the inner world, towards authentic faith. Feeling a tree as an enchanted soul, experiencing the death of ego in love, seeing rains as tears purifying the earth, realizing eternity in mother's eyes, having a deep...deep bond with the innocence of the child, the vitality of the young, the experience of the old—there is nothing Hindu or Muslim, Jew or Christian about it, there is no dogma, no institutionalized priestcraft, no Marxian 'opium of the masses', no Freudian 'collective neurosis'. This is like overcoming all sorts of blockage, and experiencing the overflow of love and energy. It has no horizons, no limits. To quote Krishnamurti once again: 'It is explosive, new, young, fresh, innocent. The innocent mind, the young mind, the mind that is extraordinarily pliable, subtle has no anchor. It is only such a mind that can experience that which you call God, that which is not measurable' (Ibid: 17). This sensitivity is true intelligence. If you spend forty years in learning mathematics but cannot look at those flowers and look at the blue sky, you are dead. However, 'if you are sensitive, which is the highest quality of intelligence, then you can look at those flowers and also study mathematics' (Ibid: 78). Indeed, knowledge restricts us; wisdom makes us fly. Knowledge makes us heavy; wisdom makes us light. Knowledge makes us afraid of death; wisdom makes us see that love is death, and death is redemption.

It is at this juncture that we need to talk about *prayer*. Can prayer be part of our everyday living, a mode of engagement with the inner world, with the cosmos? At one level, secular modernity has intensified the belief in our active 'agency'; it asserts, it wills, it performs, it achieves, it conquers. It may think that God is dead, prayer is weakness, and the quest for a transcendent experience is illusory. Yet, in this secular world we continue to see people bowing down, and praying in temples, mosques and churches. But what sort of prayer is it? Quite often, we reduce God into our own low parameters; we seek to tempt Him, bribe Him, appease Him—and we do everything for our own little comforts. And hence the prayer: 'God, find a suitable husband for my daughter, give me wealth and power, cure my illness'. In this prayer—often encouraged by astrologers, priests, the entire team of babas and gurus—I do not elevate myself, I do not change, I do not long for anything higher; instead, I remain self-centred, obsessed with myself, my little world, my comforts and pleasures. But think of a prayer of an altogether different kind: prayer as a soundless sound, prayer as the finest music, prayer as a deep longing for eternity, prayer as a journey from darkness to light, from finite to infinite, from the outer to to the inner. This prayer is not for getting a promotion, earning money, buying a new apartment; this prayer is for purifying my being, for preparing me for understanding the rhythm of life and death, for realizing the ocean inside me. Is it possible to make this prayer an integral part of our existence? How graceful it would have been had we all joined Tagore in his prayer: 'Day after day, O lord of my life, shall I stand before thee face to face. With folded hands, O lord of all worlds, shall I stand before thee face to face. Under thy great sky in solitude and silence, with humble heart shall I stand before thee face to face. In this laborious world of thine, tumultuous with toil and with struggle, among hurrying crowds shall I stand before thee face to face. And when my work shall be done in this world, O King of kings, alone and speechless shall I stand before thee face to face' (Tagore 2002: 81).

## (IX)

The kind of prayer I am talking about elevates us. But then, it may be asked: Are we capable of it? One may argue that we cannot arrive at such a higher stage of consciousness; after all, it is *fear* that is constantly restricting our horizon. How can we overcome fear? Indeed, no understanding of life is complete without looking at fear. We all have fear—fear of losing job/wealth/fame, fear of losing our loved ones, fear of separation, fear of sickness/decaying body, and above all, fear of death. This fear surrounds our existence. It would not be wrong to say that a significant part of our existence is spent in responding to this fear, and reproducing it further. We seem to be caught into the trap of fear. Take a series of revealing illustrations. I fear that I may lose all that I have earned; and hence I begin to accumulate more. However, the more I accumulate the more fearful I become; I get worried about safety and security; I get worried about others who, I fear, might have interest in my wealth. Fear leads to envy, jealousy, hatred; fear leads to the construction of the 'enemy'. In fact, it is the same psychology of fear that we see even in the politics of nation-states. A nation fears its 'enemy', manufactures destructive weapons to 'save' itself; this leads the 'enemy nation' to further add to its list of weapons. The game goes on in the name of defence, national safety, strong military base. But fear does not go. Or, for that matter, I fear that I would lose my physical vigour and beauty; I become afraid of ageing, of grey hair, of wrinkled face; and irrespective of all sorts of beauty parlour and cosmetic surgery, my fear does not vanish (imagine how pathetic film stars look when they try to avoid the natural process of ageing). Or when I think that I am primarily my body, I begin to fear its disintegration; I fear sickness; I fear that all sorts of fatal diseases might inflict me one day; I fear death. I visit the super-speciality hospital; the doctor instructs me to undergo all sorts of tests; he reminds me of the possible 'risk factors'; I begin to take medicine; the frequency of medical tests keeps increasing; I become obsessed with the body. I find myself in a cage surrounded by doctors, medical reports and insurance companies. Ivan Illich perceived this crisis so well (Illich 1988).

Never did he hesitate to say: 'Medical practice sponsors sickness by reinforcing a morbid society that encourages people to become consumers of curative, preventive, industrial and environmental medicine' and as a result, it destroys the 'potential of people to deal with their human weakness, vulnerability, and uniqueness in a personal and autonomous way' (Ibid: 41-42). With the increasing medicalization of life, 'diagnostic imperialism' is becoming a reality. 'For rich and poor', said Illich, 'life is turned into a pilgrimage through check-ups and clinics back to the ward where it started' (Ibid: 87). See our destiny. 'The life-span is brought into existence with the pre-natal check-up, when the doctor decides if and how the foetus shall be born, and it will end with a mark on a chart ordering resuscitation suspended' (Ibid: 87). All this does not make us free from the fear of death. Doctors, tests, new discoveries, and 'promises' of cure from cancer and AIDS prove to be inadequate in enabling us to overcome this fear; instead, the fear gets intensified. It is this fear that makes one incapable of understanding death, accepting its naturalness. 'The modern fear of unhygienic death', as Illich observed with great sensitivity, 'makes life appear like a race towards a terminal scramble, and man today has lost the autonomy to recognize when his time has come and to take his death into his own hands' (Ibid: 110). The medicalization of society has brought the epoch of natural death to an end. To quote Illich: 'Technical death has its own victory over dying. Mechanical death has conquered and destroyed all other deaths' (Ibid: 210).

Fear does not seem to have an end—from simple fear to the ultimate fear of death. And this fear prevents us from living this very moment, and living intensely. We become crippled. The Energy stops flowing; inspiration ceases to exist; poetry dies. What remains is the all-pervading fear—fear of others, fear of war, fear of loss and separation, fear of death. At this juncture, an important question arises: Who is fearing? What is Infinite does not fear its reduction because it cannot be reduced. What is Empty—devoid of forms—does not fear because it has got nothing to lose. The Energy that we experience all around in diverse manifestations—a mother nurturing her child, a leaf dancing, a river flowing towards the sea, an artist with her colour and canvas—is beyond fear because it is everywhere; it is in movement; it is in silence. In fact, fear is deeply related to the notion of finitude. All that is finite, limited, fragmented, temporal is filled with fear—fear of withering away, fear of disintegration. What we call 'ego' is this finite/limited/fragmented aspect of our existence. So I become my 'ego': my name, my fame, my identity, my wealth, my body. It is this ego that fears. It is limited; it is perpetually insecure; it fears its disintegration. It is this ego that fears death. My attachment to my ego makes me afraid of death. If everything that I have—wealth, power, fame—becomes useless as my body dissolves, gets reduced into dust, what remains of me? I become empty, nothing. This nothingness is horrifying. Not surprisingly, we wish to avoid death, postpone it. In a way modern medicine does it every day. From the excessively medicalized body to the life support system in the Intensive Care Unit of a super-speciality hospital—modern medicine seems to have declared war against death. Death becomes ugly, death becomes an enemy. We refuse to accept death. And as we fail to understand death we miss life.

It is at this juncture that I wish to invoke Nachiketa : his determined urge to know the meaning of death from Yama—the God of the dead. Nothing could divert him from his quest. Yama tempted him; 'I will make thee the enjoyer of thy desires. Whatever desires are hard to attain in this world of mortals, ask for all these desires at thy will...But ask not about death (KU I. 2.1). He refused to be tempted by these 'transient' objects of desire. Eventually, Yama became convinced of Nachiketa's fitness for receiving the secret of this knowledge. 'The knowing Self', said Yama, 'is never born; nor does he die at any time. He sprang from nothing and nothing sprang from him. He is unborn, eternal, abiding and primeval. He is not slain when the body is slain' (Ibid: I.2.18). We begin to realize that it is the finite body that dies; if you equate yourself with your body you fear death; but, as Nachiketa was told, 'knowing the Self who is the bodiless among bodies, the stable among the unstable, the great, the all-pervading, the wise man does not grieve' (Ibid: I.2.22). What is the nature of this Self? 'Smaller than the small, greater than the great, the Self is set in the heart of every creature' (Ibid: I.2.20).Moreover, the Self is 'without sound, without touch and without form...without test, without smell, without beginning, without end' (Ibid: I.3.15); not everyone perceives it; the small-minded go after outward pleasures, and they walk into the snare of widespread death; but 'some wise man, seeking life eternal does not seek the stable among things which are unstable here' (Ibid: II.1.2); he knows that his self, though now embodied and subject to change, is one with the imperishable omnipresent Self, and hence goes beyond all fear and sorrow. Death, as Nachiketa's story tells us, is the death of the finite, death of variations, multiple forms; but what lies hidden beneath these forms—the eternal Self—is deathless. While forms are diverse and many, the Self is One—without a beginning, without an end. 'As air which is one, entering this world becomes varied in shape according to the object it enters, so also the one Self within all beings becomes varied according to whatever it enters and also exists outside them all' (Ibid: II.2.10). To live meaningfully is to understand and realize this eternal Self. 'If one is able to perceive Him before the body falls away', Yama reminded Nachiketa, 'one would be freed from misery; if not, he becomes fit for embodiment in the created worlds' (Ibid: II.3.4). And only when self-seeking desire, ignorance and doubt disappear, such a vision is attained, and one becomes free from the fear of death.

This is like understanding that all that is finite and temporal is bound to die; and it is dying all the time. The flower that bloomed yesterday is fading away today; old leaves are falling down; the huge tide that I see right now is bound to crumble as it touches the sea shore. My ego is dying; my body is dying; my uniform is dying. However, as unbounded Energy, as Self, I am deathless because I am eternal and infinite. Recognizing myself as this Energy is like becoming a witness. As a witness, I see my body dying, I see myself changing my uniform. This is like learning the art of dying—allowing the body to let go when its turn comes, and accepting this moment with grace and gratitude. Not solely that. As it is the ego that dies, the art of dying requires the art of annihilating one's ego every moment. And the death of ego means like experiencing love—love as a fountain of Energy, love as a merger with the Eternal Self, love as a return to the mother's womb, love as an experience of what is truly deathless. That is why, this preparedness for the art of dying does not mean that we live in a pathetic state of mourning. Instead, life becomes truly enchanting and meaningful. As the body can die any time, we learn to live this very moment—with absolute intensity, gratitude and festivity. The future is uncertain; what exists is this very moment; and this moment ought to be lived as an offering, as an act of love, as an opportunity for realizing what does not die—the all-pervading Energy, and hence as a moment of fearlessness.

In this context it would not be irrelevant to mention that the *meaning* of existence we are talking about differs significantly from the orientation of Western existentialist philosophers. 'In a universe suddenly divested of illusions and lights', said Albert Camus, 'man feels alien, a stranger' (Camus in Klemke and Cahn 2008: 73). And this leads to the feeling of absurdity. The world in itself, as he would think, is not reasonable; and 'what is absurd is the confrontation of this irrational and the wild longing for clarity whose call echoes in the human heart' (Ibid: 76). Is there any meaning in all that we do, in the routine that we follow? For Camus, there seemed to be no convincing answer to this question. When this question confronts us, as Camus would have argued, a sense of meaninglessness begins to envelop us. See the way he made us reflect: 'Rising, streetcar, four hours in the office or the factory, meal, streetcar, four hours of work, meal, sleep, and Monday, Tuesday, Wednesday, Thursday, Friday and Saturday according to the same rhythm—this path is easily followed most of the time. But one day the 'why' arises and everything begins in that weariness tinged with amazement' (Ibid: 75). This weariness has 'something sickening' about it; it is likely to generate the urge to commit suicide. 'Dying voluntarily implies that you have recognized, even instinctively, the ridiculous character of that habit, the absence of any profound reason for living, the insane character of that daily agitation, and the uselessness of suffering' (Ibid: 73). Before encountering the absurd, things seem to be in place, in order. Man lives with aims, a concern for the future. 'He weighs his chances, his counts on 'some day', his retirement or the labour of his sons'; but everything becomes meaningless the moment one feels 'the absurdity of a possible death' (Ibid: 77). Death seems to be the only reality. What does life mean in such a universe—suicide or recovery? Although suicide seems to be tempting, a careful reader of Camus would admit that he was suggesting a possibility of living even amidst this absurdity. 'Knowing whether or not one can live *without appeal*, said Camus, 'is all that interests me...If I convince myself that this life has no other aspect than that of the absurd, if I feel that its whole equilibrium depends on that perpetual opposition between my conscious revolt and the darkness in which it struggles, if I admit that my freedom has no meaning except in its relation to its limited fate, then I must say that what counts is not the best of living but the most living' (Ibid: 78). This seemed to be the reason why Camus invoked Sisyphus whom the gods had condemned to ceaselessly rolling a rock to the top of a mountain, whence the stone would fall back on its own weight. See its absurdity. Sisyphus watches the stone rush down in a few moments towards that lower world whence he will have to push it up again towards the summit; he goes back down to the plain. 'It is during that return, that pause, that Sisyphus interests me'; Camus added further: 'At each of those moments when he leaves the heights and gradually sinks towards the lairs of gods, he is superior to his fate. He is stronger than his rock' (79-80). Sisyphus knows that it is absurd. Yet, he refuses to accept his defeat; he lives every moment. 'I leave Sisyphus at the foot of the mountain! One always finds one's burden again. But Sisyphus teaches the higher fidelity that negates the gods and raises rocks...The struggle itself towards the heights is enough to fill a man's heart. One must imagine Sisyphus happy' (Ibid: 81).

However, Nachiketa is qualitatively different. Sisyphus lives as a disenchanted hero; Nachiketa lives as a realized soul. Sisyphus confronts the absurd; Nachiketa sees the light. Sisyphus lives despite meaninglessness; Nachiketa lives because he finds the ultimate meaning in the realization of the Self that makes him capable of seeing death and experiencing the deathless. This is like overcoming the fear of death and realizing the deeper meaning of existence. In this context I wish to recall an incident that altered the life of Fariduddin Attar—a great medieval Sufi poet (Bayat and Jamnia 2004: 48-51). Attar was rich—the owner of a pharmacy. One day a dervish came to Attar's pharmacy for some medicine. He was amazed by the magnificence of the shop. With penetrating eyes he was looking at the shop. Not solely that. He was also scrutinizing Attar's appearance, and eventually made a strong remark: 'I am wondering how you are going to die when you have to leave all this wealth behind'. Attar felt insulted, became angry; he replied back: 'I will die just as you will'. But then, the dervish said, 'I have nothing to worry about. All I have is the cloak on my back and this *kashkul* (begging bowl). Now, do you still claim you will die the way I will'? 'Of course', Attar answered. Upon hearing this, the dervish uttered the name of God and, using his *kashkul* as a pillow, lay down and died. The incident was a turning point in Attar's life. He closed his business and withdrew into a Sufi settlement. An awakening of this kind makes us realize that when one is attached to one's ego, one's wealth, fame and position, one fears death; but when one experiences the Infinite—the abundance of love, one lives without fear; living becomes rhythmic and musical, not a confrontation with the absurd. Imagine a situation. One is alert, conscious, despite terrible bodily pain and decay. No artificial life-support system, no soulless deliberation by specialized doctors; there is only profound music, deep poetry, ecstasy and final laughter: 'I have come out of my body. I have changed my uniform. I have merged myself with the all-pervading Energy—eternal, unbounded, deathless'.

# REFERENCES


Ambedkar, B.R. 1987. *Writings and Speeches*, Vol. 3: Bombay: Education Department, Government of Maharashtra.

——, 1991. Vol. 9.

——, 1992. Vol. 11.

——, 1992. Vol. 13.

Aurobindo, Sri. 1972. 'Karmayogin' in *Early Political Writings-2*. Pondicherry: Birth Centenary Library.

——, 1977. *The Human Cycle, The Ideal of Human Unity*, and *War and Self-Determination*. Pondicherry: Sri Aurobindo Ashram.

Bauman, Zygmunt. 1989. *Modernity and the Holocaust*. London: Polity Press.

——, 2004. *Identity: Conversations with Benedetto Vecchi*. Cambridge: Polity Press.

Bayat, Mojdeh and Jamnia, Mohammad Ali. 2004. *Tales from the Land of the Sufis*. Boston: Shambhal South Asia Editions.

*Bhagavada Purana* IV. 1978. Delhi: Motilal Banarsidass.

Bose, Nirmal Kumar. 1974. *My Days with Gandhi*. Calcutta: Orient Longman.

Bougle, C. 1994. 'The Essence and Reality of the Caste System' in Gupta, Dipankar (ed.). *Social Stratification*. Delhi: Oxford University Press.

Bourdieu, Pierre. 1996. *Distinction: A Social Critique of the Judgement of Taste*. London: Routledge.

Chattopadhyay, Ratan K. 2010. *Kabuliwalla and Other Støries*. New Delhi: Orient BlackSwan.

Davis, Kingsley and Moore, Wilbert E. 1966. 'Some Principles of Stratification' in Bendix, R. and Lipset, S.M. (eds.). *Class, Status and Power: Social Stratification in Comparative Perspective*. New York: The Free Press.

Durkheim, Emile. 1969. *The Division of Labour in Society*. New York: The Free Press.

——, 2006. *Suicide: A Study in Sociology.* London and New York: Routledge.

Fanon, Frantz. 1983. *The Wretched of the Earth.* Middlesex: Penguin Books.

Foucault, Michel. 1979. *Discpline and Punish: The Birth of the Prison.* Middlesex: Penguin Books.

Freud, Sigmund. 1981. *Introductory Lectures on Psychoanalysis,* Vol. II. London: Penguin Books.

——, 2002. *Leonardo da Vinci: A Memory of His Childhood.* London: Routledge.

Fromm, Erich. 1982. *To Have or To Be.* London: Abacus.

Gandhi, M.K. 1976. *An Autobiography or the Story of My Experiments with Truth.* Ahmedabad: Navajivan Press.

——, 1989. *Hind Swaraj or Indian Home Rule.* Ahmedabad: Navajivan Publishing House.

Gerth, H.H. and Mills, C. Wright (eds.). 1946. *From Max Weber: Essays in Sociology.* New York: Oxford University Press.

Gramsci, Antonio. 1971. *Selections from the Prison Notebooks.* London: Lawrence and Wishart.

Goffman, E. 1959. *The Presentation of Self in Everyday Life.* New York: Doubleday Anchor.

Hasan, Khalid (ed.). *Bitter Fruit: The Very Best of Saadat Hasan Manto.* New Delhi: Penguin Books.

Ibsen, Henrik. 2005. *A Doll's House.* Dodo Press.

Illich, Ivan. 1988. *Limits to Medicine, Medical Nemesis: The Expropriation of Health.* London: Penguin Books.

Jalil, Rakshanda (tr.). 2011. *The Best of Premchand: The Temple and the Mosque.* Noida: Harper Perennial.

Jamal, Mahmood (tr.). 2009. *Islamic Mystical Poetry: Sufi Verse from the Mystics to Rumi.* London: Penguin Books.

Kafka, Franz. 1982. *The Trial.* Middlesex: Penguin Books.

Kakar, Sudhir. 1982. *The Inner World: A Psychoanalytic Study of Childhood and Society in India.* Delhi: Oxford University Press.

Khanam, Farida (ed.) 2012. *The Quran.* New Delhi: Goodword Books.

Khusrau, Amir. 2011. *In the Bazaar of Love: The Selected Poetry of Amir Khusrau.* New Delhi: Penguin Books.

Klemke, E.D. and Cahn, Steven M. 2008.*The Meaning of Life: A Reader.* New York: Oxford University Press.

Krishnamurti, Jiddu. 2006. *Krishnamurti on Education*. Chennai: Krishnamurti Foundation of India.

Marcuse, Herbert. 2002. *One-Dimensional Man: Studies in the Ideology of Advanced Industrial Society*. London and New York: Routledge.

Marx, Karl. 1977. *Economic and Philosophic Manuscripts of 1844*. Moscow: Progress Publishers.

Marx, Karl and Engels, Fredrick. 1976. *The German Ideology*. Moscow: Progress Publishers.

——, 2012. *The Manifesto of the Communist Party*. New Delhi: People's Publishing House.

Murti, V.V. Ramana (ed.). 1970. *Gandhi: Essential Writings*. New Delhi: Gandhi Peace Foundation.

Parsons, Talcott. 1949. *The Structure of Social Action: A Study in Social Theory with Special Reference to a Group of Recent European Writers*. Glencoe/Illinois: The Free Press.

——, 1951. *The Social System*. Glencoe/Illinois: The Free Press.

——, (ed.). 1964. *Max Weber; The Theory of Social and Economic Organization*. New York: The Free Press.

*Rabindranath Tagore Omnibus I*. 2011. New Delhi: Rupa Publications India Private Limited.

Radhakrishnan, S. 1953. *The Principal Upanishads*. London: George Allen and Unwin Ltd.

——, 1976. *The Bhagavad Gita*. Bombay: Blackie and Sons Ltd.

Schumacher, E.F. 1980. *Good Work*. London: Abacus.

Shastri, J.L (ed.). 1970. *The Shiva Purana*, Vol. I. Delhi: Motilal Banarsidass.

Sheridan, Alan. 1980. *Michel Foucault: The Will to Truth*. London and New York: Tavistock Publications.

Tagore, Rabindranath. 1925. 'Red Oleanders': Author's Introduction' in *Visva Quarterly*, October, 1925.

——, 1961. *Towards Universal Man*. Calcutta: Asia Publishing House.

——, 1985. *Nationalism*. Madras: Macmillan.

——, 2002. *Gitanjali*. New Delhi: Indialog Publications Pvt. Ltd.

Vivekananda, Swami. 1989. *The Complete Works of Swami Vivekananda*, Vol. IV. Calcutta: Advaita Ashram.

# Index